7 Successful
Stock Market Strategies

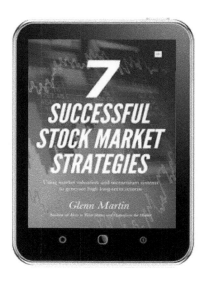

7 Successful Stock Market Strategies

Using market valuation and momentum systems to generate high long-term returns

Glenn Martin

HARRIMAN HOUSE LTD

18 College Street

Petersfield

Hampshire

GU31 4AD

GREAT BRITAIN

Tel: +44 (0)1730 233870

Email: contact@harriman-house.com

Website: www.harriman-house.com

First published in Great Britain in 2015

Paperback ISBN: 9780857194626

eBook ISBN: 9780857194633

British Library Cataloguing in Publication Data

A CIP catalogue record for this book can be obtained from the British Library.

CONTENTS

About the author   ix

Risk and copyright warnings   x

Acknowledgements   xi

Preface   xiii
  Why I wrote this book   xiii
  UK equities   xiv
    Why invest in UK equities?   xiv
    How to invest in UK equities   xiv
  What's new   xv
  Who this book is for   xvii
  Who this book is not for   xvii
  How this book is structured   xviii
  How to use this book   xx

PART A. BACKGROUND THEORY   1

Chapter 1. Risks and Returns   3
  Why it is riskier to invest in cash than in the FTSE 100 or FTSE 250 over
    the long term   3
    The nature of long-term risk   3
    Inflation   4
    Why long-term returns from equities beat those of cash deposits   5
  Comparative risks and returns for different investment strategies   5
  Explaining the risks and returns of each strategy   7
    Cash   7
    Strategy 1a. Long-term investment in the FTSE 100   7
    Strategy 1b. Long-term investment in the FTSE 100, with freefall exits   8
    Strategy 2a. Long-term investment in the FTSE 250   8
    Strategy 2b. Long-term investment in the FTSE 250, with freefall exits   9
    Strategy 3. Long-term investment in the FTSE 100, with market timing   9
    Strategy 4. Long-term investment in the FTSE 250, with market timing   10
    Strategy 5. Long-term FTSE 100 spread trading strategy   10
    Strategy 6. Long-term FTSE 250 spread trading strategy   11
  Prospective future returns   12

Chapter 2. UK Stock Market Valuation System   15
  The principles for valuing the FTSE 100   15
    The sources of value   15

Measuring value effectively   16
A five-year investment period   17
Dividends at the heart of the process   17
The detailed steps to determine current value   18
Creating a spreadsheet to value the FTSE 100   19
Setting up the spreadsheet template   20
Inputting data into the template   21
Inputting formulae into the template to get results   27
Extending the spreadsheet to personalise investment growth   33
Inputting data   34
Inputting formulae into the template to get results   36
The two main uses of FTSE 100 valuations   39
1. When to buy and sell   40
2. Comparing five-year investment returns with other investments   46

Chapter 3. Adding Market Momentum To The Valuation System   **51**
Using Digital Look to construct moving average charts for the FTSE 100   52
Market Momentum System: Example 1   53
Market Momentum System: Example 2   55
Complete record of the Market Momentum System for the FTSE 100
and FTSE 250   56

PART B. SEVEN STRATEGIES   **59**

Chapter 4. Strategy 1 – Long-Term Investment In The FTSE 100   **61**
How to maintain a long-term investment in the FTSE 100   62
Disadvantages of unit trust and OEIC investments   63
Maintaining an investment using an ETF   63
Choosing the right FTSE 100 ETF   64
Long-term historic returns of cost-effective investment in the FTSE 100   65
Prospective future returns from this strategy   66
Get a FTSE 100 valuation before you invest   67
Summary of the strategy   68
Strategy 1b. Boosting your returns and reducing your risk   68

Chapter 5. Strategy 2 – Long-Term Investment In The FTSE 250   **71**
How to maintain a long-term investment in the FTSE 250   72
Choosing the right FTSE 250 ETF   72
Long-term historic returns of cost-effective investment in the FTSE 250   73
Prospective future returns from this strategy   74
Get a FTSE 100 valuation before you invest   75
Summary of the strategy   76
Strategy 2b. Boosting your returns and reducing your risk   76

Chapter 6. Strategy 3 – Boosting Long-Term Investment In The FTSE 100 With Market Timing   **79**

Overlap between the Market Momentum System and the Stock Market Valuation System   80

Summary of the strategy   80

Track record of the strategy   81

   Assumptions   83

Future performance prospects   84

Chapter 7. Strategy 4 – Boosting Long-Term Investment In The FTSE 250 With Market Timing   **85**

Overlap between the Market Momentum System and the Stock Market Valuation System   86

Summary of the strategy   86

Track record of the strategy   87

   Assumptions   89

Future performance prospects   89

Chapter 8. Strategy 5 – Long-Term FTSE 100 Financial Spread Trading Strategy   **91**

What are financial spread trades?   91

   Financial spread trade example   91

   What is an equity future and how are the prices derived?   92

The advantages of financial spread trading   93

The potential disadvantages of financial spread trading   93

The key decision elements of financial spread trading   94

The FTSE 100 spread trading strategy   94

   Key success drivers for the strategy   94

   Summary of the strategy (gearing multiple of 7 and 27.5% stop-loss)   95

   Risk controls of this strategy   96

   Executing the strategy in detail (gearing multiple of 7 and 27.5% stop-loss)   97

   Track record of the strategy (gearing multiple of 7 and stop-loss of 27.5%)   101

Optimising gearing multiples and stop-loss levels   107

FTSE 100 spread trading strategy simulation tool   108

   Example of using the tool for gearing and stop-loss levels of 7 and 95% respectively   108

   Growth of the fund   109

   Using the simulator to test the impact of different gearing and stop-loss levels   110

   Preventing stop-losses at different gearing levels   110

   Trying other combinations of gearing and stop-loss levels   111

   Setting different gearing and stop-loss levels   112

Chapter 9. Strategy 6 – Long-Term FTSE 250 Spread Trading Strategy   **115**

Executing the strategy in detail (gearing multiple of 7 and 27.5% stop-loss)   116

Trade entry and exit dates   120

Track record of the strategy   120

Using different gearing multiples and stop-loss levels   120

Chapter 10. Strategy 7 – Running A Tax-Efficient FTSE 100 Tracker Through Spread Trading   **121**

The basic steps to create the synthetic FTSE 100 tracker   121

Financial comparison   123

Assumptions   124

Conclusions   127

Notes on the calculations (in order of the fields)   127

PART C. PRACTICAL CONSIDERATIONS   **131**

Introduction   **133**

Choosing the right investment vehicle for each strategy   **135**

Strategies 1 and 2 – Long-term investment in the FTSE 100 and FTSE 250   135

Strategies 3 and 4 – Boosting long-term investment in the FTSE 100 and FTSE 250 with market timing   136

Strategies 5 and 6 – Long-term FTSE 100 and FTSE 250 spread trading strategies   137

Strategy 7   137

Recommended service providers   **139**

ISAs   139

SIPPs   139

Online Share account (non ISA)   140

Instant-access cash account(s)   140

Spread trading firm   140

Tax information   **141**

EPILOGUE   **143**

APPENDIX – GLOSSARY OF TERMS   **145**

ABOUT THE AUTHOR

After graduating from Wadham College, Oxford, Glenn Martin started a career in the City. Over a period of 34 years he worked for a number of financial institutions. For the latter part of this career he worked as Chief Information Officer for investment banks. In 2004 he won the Banking Technology Award for the Best IT Operational Achievement.

As a successful private investor, in 1994 Glenn developed a system for calculating the intrinsic value of the FTSE 100 and of individual UK shares. The system proved reliable and in 2006 he established ShareMaestro Limited to package and promote it. ShareMaestro (www.sharemaestro.co.uk) was then launched commercially in 2007 and since then has received very positive reviews in the financial press. The *Daily Telegraph's* Tom Stevenson said: "ShareMaestro ticks all the right boxes in my holy grail quest."

Glenn's first book, *How to Value Shares and Outperform the Market,* was published by Harriman House in 2011.

After his family and investment, Glenn's main interests are tennis, travel and drumming.

RISK AND COPYRIGHT WARNINGS

Investment in equities and stock markets involves risk. Past performance is not necessarily a guide to future performance. Your specific needs, investment objectives and financial situation need to be taken into account before making investment decisions. You are strongly recommended to take appropriate professional advice before acting on any information or valuations provided directly or indirectly by this book and to conduct your investment activity through an appropriately authorised company. Every possible effort has been made to ensure that the information in this book is accurate at the time of writing and the Publisher and Author cannot accept responsibility for any errors or omissions. No responsibility for any direct or indirect loss occasioned to any person or corporate body acting or refraining to act as a result of reading material in this book can be accepted by the Editor, the Publisher or the Author.

ACKNOWLEDGEMENTS

The valuation systems described in this book are based on ShareMaestro, which I launched commercially in 2007. Without the help of several key supporters, ShareMaestro would never have become available to private investors and this book would never have been written.

Firstly, I want to recognise the great work done by Zahir Virani, who turned what was a pretty crude spreadsheet into a great piece of software and who has managed subsequent enhancements very professionally. Next comes Dominic Picarda, formerly Associate Editor of the *Investors Chronicle*. Dominic has been a constant ally. He helped me tremendously with the validation of ShareMaestro, always asks thought-provoking questions and wrote some great articles on ShareMaestro for readers of the *Investors Chronicle*.

Tom Stevenson, whilst working at the *Daily Telegraph*, had the courage to headline and showcase ShareMaestro, then an unknown system, in the business section of the paper. It is extremely rare for articles on investment software to feature in the business pages of the broadsheets. Tom's article was both shrewd and positive; it sealed the launch of ShareMaestro.

Tim Clarke, General Manager of ShareScope, has also been a great ally. He masterminded the collaboration between ShareScope and ShareMaestro, through which ShareScope provides data to ShareMaestro. He has also kindly given permission for ShareScope graphs to be used in this book.

Annabel Watson is my model private investor. As well as acting as my guinea pig for new versions of ShareMaestro, she has put a lot of effort into the presentational side of the product. She is also a great source of inspiration.

Chris Tiernan, Managing Partner of Grosvenor Consultancy Services LLP, has devoted a huge amount of effort to this book, which he has helped me edit, and to the validation of the strategies used. His attention to detail and constant patience are exemplary.

My final acknowledgement is to my family, who provide constant encouragement and put up with my obsession to motivate private investors to manage their own funds.

February 2015

PREFACE

Why I wrote this book

We live in a very uncertain world and I believe that everyone should maximise the returns on their savings in order to have a robust source of finance for all contingencies.

For this reason, I do not want you to entrust your long-term savings to banks or building societies. My mission in this book is to explain how my seven successful UK stock market strategies could make you far more money. You might even be able to retire early.

The maximum compound annual return on cash savings over the last 30 years has been 4.1%, after the deduction of basic rate UK income tax. By contrast, my strategies have achieved annual returns ranging between 9.2% and 36.9%, again after the deduction of basic rate tax.

Because of the magic of compounding returns, small differences in annual returns make huge differences in the size of long-term savings pots. Even the lowest annual return delivered by one of the strategies – 9.2% – would, compounded over 30 years, generate a savings pot over quadruple the size of the cash savings pot (4.1% compounded over 30 years). The highest annual long-term strategy return of 36.9% would generate a savings pot nearly 3,700 times the size of the cash savings pot. For example, £1000 invested at a compound annual return of 4.1% will produce a savings pot after 30 years of £3,338, compared with a pot of £12,362,418 delivered by a compound annual return of 36.9% over the same period.

The current environment of low interest rates – the UK base rate has been held at an historic low of 0.5% since March 2009 – increases the comparative advantages of the strategies still further. The returns from investing long-term in cash accounts have been severely reduced by this period of low interest rates, which puts even greater value on the returns that can be delivered by investing in the UK stock market.

I believe that most savers shun the UK stock market because they think that it is excessively risky, would take too much effort and, anyway, they don't understand it. This book aims to address all those concerns.

I will show why investing in the UK stock market is less risky than investing long-term savings in cash deposits, providing you have a proven strategy with effective risk controls.

I will also explain in very simple terms how it is extremely easy to invest in the UK stock market. The maximum effort required for any of the strategies is one hour per week, but most of them require considerably less time than this. In my view, devoting up to one hour a week to achieving long-term financial security is a very sensible use of your time. It is also quite enjoyable.

UK equities

Why invest in UK equities?

Over the very long term (20 years upwards), UK equities have delivered higher returns than any other non-physical asset class (gilts, bonds and cash).[1] I prefer UK equities over international equities since the latter carry an extra layer of risk – namely, exchange rate risk. Adverse movements of the foreign currency against the pound sterling could erode or even eliminate any gains made in the value of foreign investments. So, this book focuses on investing in the UK stock market.

How to invest in UK equities

If you want to invest in the UK stock market, you have three main options:

1. Investing in individual UK shares.

2. Investing in an actively managed commercial UK equity fund, in which a fund manager chooses shares which he hopes will outperform the market.

3. Investing in a tracker fund, which aims to match the performance of the FTSE 100 or FTSE 250 index.

---

1   Source: Barclays Capital 2014 Equity Gilt Study

Investing in individual UK shares requires a lot of effort, but can be very rewarding. In *How to Value Shares and Outperform the Market* (Harriman House, 2011), I explained how you can build a spreadsheet to identify the intrinsic value of a specific share. Alternatively, the ShareMaestro software (www.sharemaestro.co.uk) provides weekly automated valuations for shares in the FTSE All-Share index.

To control the risk of individual share investment, you need to run a portfolio of at least ten shares. But there is still a risk that some shares will damage the performance of the portfolio for unpredictable reasons. For example, BP and Tesco were both highly rated companies until incidents appeared out of the blue which led to a collapse in their share prices. This book is aimed at investors who have limited time to spend on stock market investing, so the strategies do not include individual share investment.

Coming to the second option, statistically most UK equity funds do not outperform the market. Indeed, logically they could not do so because they constitute most of the market. Their high fees ensure that the average fund will in fact underperform the market. The strategies in this book therefore do not include the use of actively managed UK equity funds.

The amounts invested in tracker funds, such as ETFs, have grown enormously in recent years due to disappointment with the performance of actively managed funds. There is a lot of competition between the providers of these funds and consequently their annual fees have fallen to the point where they are considerably lower than those charged by actively managed funds. With the exception of the spread trading strategies (see the glossary in the Appendix for explanations of technical terms), all the strategies in this book involve the use of tracker funds. Most of the strategies use techniques to outperform the tracker funds and to control risk effectively. I also recommend the most cost-effective tracker funds, as there are different ways in which these funds are packaged.

What's new

This book uses the same core successful Stock Market Valuation System as my previous book, *How to Value Shares and Outperform the Market*. However, I have introduced some improvements and made the System easier to use. The new features in this book are as follows:

- The spreadsheet for the Stock Market Valuation System has been extended to include personalised investment returns, which take into account your personal income tax and capital gains tax rates.

- Access is given to a private page of the ShareMaestro website, which gives my current assessment of the key prospective real dividend growth rate for the FTSE 100.

- I have modified the moving averages used in the Market Momentum System to use 100 day and 200 day simple moving averages. These are commonly used moving averages and replace the previously used 142 day and 245 day moving averages, since these could be accused of having been cherry-picked to fit with past events (which they were not). The Market Momentum System identifies when you should exit the market, if it is in freefall, and when you should re-enter the market.

- The FTSE 100 market timing strategy has been modified to include Market Momentum exits and re-entries as well as buy and sell signals from the Stock Market Valuation System. This change has increased returns as well as enhancing risk control.

- A FTSE 250 market timing strategy has been introduced. This also includes the Market Momentum System, which uses the moving averages of prices from the FTSE 250 rather than from the FTSE 100. I have also provided the track record of this strategy since 1984.

- I have provided the 30-year track record of a simple buy and hold strategy for both the FTSE 100 and FTSE 250.

- I have also provided details of the increased performance of the above simple buy and hold strategy that would be achieved by incorporating the Market Momentum System (but not the Stock Market Valuation System buy and sell signals).

- In *How to Value Shares and Outperform the Market,* I outlined a possible spread trading strategy which could be used to provide enhanced returns on FTSE 100 investments. I have now extensively researched this strategy and provide both the details of how to execute it and the long-term track record. The historic returns from this strategy are stellar.

- Access is provided to a FTSE 100 spread trading simulator on the ShareMaestro website. This simulator enables you to test what historic returns you would have achieved according to your appetite for risk. You can also see the fluctuation in the spread trade fund values, as every trade since 1984 is listed.

- I supply details of a strategy which provides a synthetic holding in the FTSE 100 through a combination of an instant-access cash account and quarterly spread trades in the FTSE 100. This strategy has the major advantage that it creates a tax-free holding, since spread trading profits are exempt from capital gains tax and no higher rate tax is payable on dividends, which are built into the spread trading prices.

Who this book is for

This book is for anyone who wants a more secure financial future – especially those who cannot rely on future earnings for a comfortable life. This book is also for anyone who wants to take control of their own financial affairs.

To secure your financial future, you must be prepared to:

- Invest up to one hour per week of your time.

- Have an investment horizon of at least five years.

- Accept some risk and not be easily panicked by short-term events, in exchange for the reasonable expectation of significantly higher longer-term rewards.

Who this book is not for

This is not for those investors who:

- Believe there is a silver bullet which will guarantee instant riches. **These guaranteed silver bullets do not exist.**

- Trust tipsters or fund managers who, by the use of highly selective examples, give the impression that regular returns exceeding 30% p.a. can be easily obtained (for a fee!). The only professionals who abuse statistics as much as politicians are financial product salesmen. **If an investment proposition sounds too good to be true, it almost certainly is too good to be true.**

- Are short-term traders who expect to make their fortunes in a few months. **Virtually all non-professional short-term traders lose money. My strategies are for investors who target long-term profits rather than for traders, who aim to make a quick buck.**

- Cannot adopt a systematic and disciplined approach. **Whilst not much effort is required, it is essential that you follow in detail the rules of each strategy.**

- Need access to their investment within five years. **Fluctuations in market prices may reduce the value of the initial investment within that timescale.**

- Are not comfortable with basic mathematics.

How this book is structured

Part A gives the background theory underpinning the strategies:

- Chapter 1 provides a brief description of each strategy, together with the associated risks and the long-term returns achieved since 1984.

- Chapter 2 explains in detail how you can build a spreadsheet to provide a current intrinsic valuation of the FTSE 100, together with the projected investment returns for a five-year investment. This is called the Stock Market Valuation System. This chapter also provides long-term validation of the accuracy of the valuations and describes how the valuations can be used as buy and sell signals. Evidence is also provided as to how these FTSE 100 buy and sell signals can be used effectively for the FTSE 250.

- Chapter 3 describes a key risk control system, using simple moving averages of prices, for selling the FTSE 100 or FTSE 250 when the market is in freefall and re-entering the market when it has stabilised. This is called the Market Momentum System. In addition to controlling risk, historically this system has increased returns.

Part B provides a detailed explanation of how to operate each strategy, together with each strategy's long-term track record since 1984:

- Strategy 1 involves buying and passively holding the FTSE 100. Dividends are reinvested in the FTSE 100. I also cover a variation of this strategy, which involves additionally exiting and re-entering the market according to signals from the Market Momentum System.

- Strategy 2 involves buying and passively holding the FTSE 250. Dividends are reinvested in the FTSE 250. The FTSE 250 includes the next 250 largest companies after the FTSE 100. I also cover a variation of this strategy which involves additionally exiting and re-entering the market according to signals from the Market Momentum System.

- Strategy 3 involves switching investment between the FTSE 100 and instant-access cash according to both the buy and sell signals from the Stock Market Valuation System and the exit and re-entry signals from the Market Momentum System. The resulting returns have been significantly higher than from a passive holding in the FTSE 100 (Strategy 1).

- Strategy 4 involves switching investment between the FTSE 250 and instant-access cash according to both the buy and sell signals from the Stock Market Valuation System and the exit and re-entry signals from the Market Momentum System. The resulting returns have been significantly higher than from a passive holding in the FTSE 250 (Strategy 2).

- Strategy 5 involves holding an instant-access cash account and buying/selling quarterly FTSE 100 spread trades according to both the buy and sell signals from the Stock Market Valuation System and the exit and re-entry signals from the Market Momentum System. Profits and losses from each trade are transferred between the spread trading cash account and the instant-access cash account. The short-term risk of this strategy is very high, but the long-term rewards are potentially stellar. I explain the key concepts of spread trading and how you can choose your own level of risk and reward. I have provided access to a spread trading simulator to help you make the choice.

- Strategy 6 is similar to Strategy 5, except that investment is made in FTSE 250 spread trades. The Market Momentum System uses moving averages of FTSE 250 prices. The long-term returns from this strategy are potentially even higher than for the FTSE 100 spread trade strategy, because the growth of the FTSE 250 price has historically been much higher than that of the FTSE 100 price. However, the short-term risks are also higher since the spread between the buying and selling prices of FTSE 250 spread trades is much wider than that of FTSE 100 spread trades. The detailed track record of this strategy is not provided because of uncertainty about the historic spreads.

- Strategy 7 explains how you can construct a synthetic FTSE 100 tracker by investing in FTSE 100 spread trades and holding an instant-access cash account. This requires a disciplined approach but the great benefit is that the synthetic holding will be free of capital gains tax under current UK tax law and also free of higher rate tax on the dividends which are included in the FTSE 100 spread trade prices.

Part C, Practical Considerations, provides practical information on what you need to operate each of the strategies.

I recommend the most appropriate investment vehicle for each strategy. I also give information on service providers that I have found to be cost-effective and service-oriented.

Finally, a glossary of technical terms is provided in the Appendix.

How to use this book

Ideally you should read this book from cover to cover. You should then decide whether you wish to use any of these strategies and, if so, which ones.

However, I appreciate that we all have busy lives and that you may not have time to read the whole book. If so, I suggest that you first read Part A, Chapter 1 on Risks and Returns. This gives brief details of how each strategy operates, the amount of effort required, plus the associated risks and returns. You should then choose which strategy or strategies interest you:

- If you choose the variations on Strategy 1 and Strategy 2, which include market momentum (1b and 2b), you should read Part A, Chapter 3 on the Market Momentum System.

- If you choose Strategy 3 or Strategy 4, you should read Part A, Chapter 2 on the Stock Market Valuation System and Part A, Chapter 3 on the Market Momentum System. If you do not wish to build the spreadsheet described in Chapter 2, you can subscribe to ShareMaestro, which provides automated weekly valuations of the FTSE 100, together with the personalised investment returns.

- If you wish to use a synthetic FTSE 100 tax-free tracker for Strategy 1 or Strategy 3, you should read the chapter in Part B on Strategy 7.

Whichever strategy you choose, you should read Part C on Practical Considerations. This provides advice on the best investment vehicle for each strategy and recommendations on service providers.

If you are unfamiliar with any of the terms used in this book, please refer to the glossary of technical terms in the Appendix.

PART A.
BACKGROUND THEORY

CHAPTER 1. RISKS AND RETURNS

Why it is riskier to invest in cash than in the FTSE 100 or FTSE 250 over the long term

The nature of long-term risk

Most people in the UK invest their long-term savings in cash deposits, perhaps thinking this is less risky than investing in equities. After all, most people can remember the 1987 hurricane crash or the collapse which followed the bursting of the dot.com bubble, can't they? However, these investors are wrong, for two reasons:

1. They are confusing short-term risk with long-term risk.

2. They misunderstand the nature of investment risk.

Investors who put their long-term savings in cash because of concerns about short-term risk are decimating their long-term savings. Clearly, if you are saving for a short-term objective, you **do** need to be concerned about short-term risk. However, if you are saving for the long term (e.g. for a retirement pension), then you ought to be concerned with long-term risk. In this case, confusing short-term risk with long-term risk is a fatal error. In this context I am defining short term as up to five years and long term as over five years.

Risk is the probability of something bad happening. The higher the probability, the higher the risk. The nature of the risk depends on the context. So the main risk when skiing is the potential for crashing. The main risk when walking a tightrope without a safety net between tower blocks in Chicago is that of falling off the rope.

What is the risk associated with long-term investing?

My definition is: the risk of achieving a poor or even negative annual real return. The real return is the actual return less inflation. Most long-term cash investors do not realise that, if your cash savings have increased in value by 50% when inflation has increased by 80%, you have actually lost money in real terms. In other words, you have made a negative real return.

Inflation

In the UK, there are various measures of inflation, depending on the selection of goods and services for which the prices are measured. The standard measure of inflation used to be the Retail Prices Index (RPI), but UK governments have increasingly used the Consumer Price Index (CPI) as their preferred measure.

It is no coincidence that the CPI is normally lower than the RPI – as a result, the use of this measure maximises tax revenues and minimises what the government has to pay out in inflation-linked benefits. The CPI excludes major items of expenditure incurred by most households – e.g. mortgage interest. I have used RPI to calculate the real returns of the strategies covered in this book, as it is a more realistic measure.

When I say "real return", I mean the return in excess of inflation. When I refer to "actual return", I mean the actual return achieved, including inflation. When inflation is positive, i.e. prices are rising, the actual return will always be higher than the real return.

As I will show in the next section, over the last 30 years the FTSE 100 and FTSE 250 have achieved considerably higher real returns than cash deposits. And if you look at most five-year periods within the 30 years, the real return from cash deposits has underperformed that of the UK stock market. If you want to compare the returns for an even longer period, say 50 years, UK equities have achieved over triple the real annual return of cash deposits.

It is worth mentioning that, by cash deposits, I mean cash invested in banks and building societies. I do not mean government bonds (gilts) or corporate bonds. The prices of bonds generally fluctuate according to the level of interest rates. They tend to perform well when interest rates are falling and badly when interest rates are rising.

It is therefore probable that, over the long term, UK equities will deliver a much higher real return than cash. Consequently it is riskier to invest long term in cash rather than in UK equities.

Why long-term returns from equities beat those of cash deposits

There is a very simple reason why long-term returns from equities tend to be higher than those from cash deposits. Banks and building societies need to attract deposits in order to lend money to borrowers. They make profits from the difference between the rates they give to depositors and the rates they charge borrowers. Consequently, they are motivated to provide the minimum level of interest necessary to attract depositors in order to maximise their profits.

The motivation of the executives of companies whose shares (equities) are traded on the UK stock market is quite different. They want to maximise the share price because most of them hold stock or stock options in the companies which employ them. Firstly, they want to improve the profits of the company to make it attractive to investors. Secondly, they are keen to increase dividends, partly because they own shares in the company and partly because a good dividend record supports growth in the share price. Even if the managers do not own shares in their company, they are still motivated to increase profits (from which dividends are paid) because their jobs, salaries and bonuses depend on it.

So, in a nutshell, human motivation drives greater real returns from equities than from cash.

Comparative risks and returns for different investment strategies

Table 1 shows the comparative returns, risk and effort for the various investment strategies covered in this book. The returns, risk and effort for cash deposits are included as a benchmark.

After the table I will explain the rationale of the risk and effort ratings for each strategy. Because of the mathematics of compounding returns over many years, a small difference in annual return will make a large difference in fund size many years later.

The quoted returns are net of UK basic rate tax. They do not include any allowance for capital gains tax, as this depends on individual circumstances. Capital gains tax will not be payable if the investment is held within a tax-free vehicle or if one of the spread trading strategies is used. The calculation of the returns is explained in the relevant section on each strategy.

The returns shown are the actual returns stripped of inflation (i.e. they are the real returns). The actual annual long-term returns for the strategies range from

9.2% to 36.9%, considerably higher than the maximum actual return of 4.1% achieved by cash.

The number ratings, on a scale from 1 to 5, allow the strategies to be compared with each other. For example, the effort required for all the strategies is fairly small. The highest effort rating of 5 is given to the spread trading strategy, but the actual effort required is a maximum of one hour per week.

Strategy 7 is not included in the table as it is not an investment strategy with a long-term return, but a strategy for an investment vehicle.

TABLE 1. REAL RETURNS, RISK AND EFFORT FOR THE INVESTMENT STRATEGIES

Investment strategy, 1/1/84 to 30/09/14	Long-term real return (% pa)	Long-term risk	Short-term risk	Effort
Cash	Up to 1.2	5	1	1
Strategy 1a. Long-term investment in the FTSE 100	5.5	3	4	1
Strategy 1b. As 1a but with freefall exit	6.2	2.5	3	2
Strategy 2a. Long-term investment in the FTSE 250	7.4	3	4	1
Strategy 2b. As 2a but with freefall exit	7.9	2.5	3	2
Strategy 3. Long-term investment in the FTSE 100 with market timing	6.6	2	3	3
Strategy 4. Long-term investment in the FTSE 250 with market timing	8.4	2	3	3
Strategy 5. Long-term FTSE 100 spread trading	up to 32.2	3	5	5
Strategy 6. Long-term FTSE 250 spread trading	Long-term record not provided due to unavailability of information on long-term spreads.			

Key: the scale 1 to 5 ranges from 1 low to 5 high. (The FTSE 250 strategies start on 1/1/86.)

Explaining the risks and returns of each strategy

Cash

Long-term real annual return	Up to 1.2%
Long-term risk	5
Short-term risk	1
Effort	1

This strategy involves placing a series of cash deposits. The highest interest rates are normally available for long-term fixed deposits. The maximum term is normally five years. However, you need to be careful to avoid locking your money into an account with a low interest rate when interest rates are rising. If you can lock into high interest rates when interest rates are falling, so much the better.

The real annual return will vary according to the length of the deposit period. Long-term risk is high because, over long periods, cash has historically underperformed all other major asset classes. The risk is especially high when inflation is rising. The short-term risk is low because the initial investment sum will not fall in nominal terms, even if other asset classes are crashing. The effort required is low and is restricted to renewing maturing deposits and ensuring, as far as possible, that the deposits with each institution having a separate banking licence do not exceed the £85,000 FSCS (Financial Services Compensation Scheme) compensation limit should the institution fail.

Strategy 1a. Long-term investment in the FTSE 100

Long-term real annual return	5.5%
Long-term risk	3
Short-term risk	4
Effort	1

This strategy involves placing lump sum investments in FTSE 100 tracker funds and letting the investments grow until needed. This strategy depends on all dividends being reinvested in the fund.

The long-term risk is medium because the strategy involves passive investment in the FTSE 100 and there is no protection against market crashes. The short-term risk is relatively high because of the potential of a market crash. The effort required is very low – less than five minutes per week – since, once the investment is made, the only requirement is to make annual tax returns, if applicable, and also to top up the investment if additional funds become available.

Strategy 1b. Long-term investment in the FTSE 100, with freefall exits

Long-term real annual return	6.2%
Long-term risk	2.5
Short-term risk	3
Effort	2

This is a variation of Strategy 1a. The only difference is that you sell your FTSE 100 investment when the market is in freefall and re-enter the market when it has stabilised. This technique is detailed in Chapter 3, Adding Market Momentum to the Valuation System.

The long-term and short-term risks are lower than 1a, because you should avoid the worst impact of severe market crashes. The extra effort involved is minimal because the market momentum exit signals happen so rarely. Funds are placed in instant-access cash deposits when the FTSE 100 investment is not held.

Strategy 2a. Long-term investment in the FTSE 250

Long-term real annual return	7.4%
Long-term risk	3
Short-term risk	4
Effort	1

This strategy involves placing lump sum investments in FTSE 250 tracker funds and letting the investments grow until needed. This strategy depends on all dividends being reinvested in the fund.

The long-term risk is medium because the strategy involves passive investment in the FTSE 250 and there is no protection against market crashes. The short-term risk is relatively high because of the potential impact of market crashes. The effort required is very low – less than 5 minutes per week – since, once the investment is made, the only requirement is to make annual tax returns, if applicable, and also to top up the investment if additional funds become available.

Strategy 2b. Long-term investment in the FTSE 250, with freefall exits

Long-term real annual return	7.9%
Long-term risk	2.5
Short-term risk	3
Effort	2

This is a variation of Strategy 2a. The only difference is that you sell your FTSE 250 investment when the market is in freefall and re-enter the market when it has stabilised. This technique is detailed in Chapter 3, Adding Market Momentum to the Valuation System.

The long-term and short-term risks are lower than 2a because you should avoid the worst impact of severe market crashes. The extra effort involved is minimal because these market momentum exit signals happen so rarely. Funds are placed in instant-access cash deposits when the FTSE 250 investment is not held.

Strategy 3. Long-term investment in the FTSE 100, with market timing

Long-term real annual return	6.6%
Long-term risk	2
Short-term risk	3
Effort	3

With this strategy, you switch investment between a FTSE 100 tracker fund and cash deposits according to the buy and sell signals from the Stock Market

Valuation System described in Chapter 2. You also exit and re-enter the FTSE 100 according to the Market Momentum System.

The long-term risk of this strategy is relatively low because you should only be invested in the FTSE 100 when it is good value and you should also be disinvested when the market is in freefall. The effort is relatively high because you need to perform a weekly valuation of the FTSE 100, place limit orders to sell or buy when target sell or buy prices are triggered and you need to follow the Market Momentum System. However, the total effort should be no more than 30 minutes per week. Short-term risk is relatively high because you may suffer short-term losses if market conditions worsen sharply.

Strategy 4. Long-term investment in the FTSE 250, with market timing

Long-term real annual return	8.4%
Long-term risk	2
Short-term risk	3
Effort	3

This is the same as Strategy 3, except that investment is made in the FTSE 250 rather than in the FTSE 100. The buy and sell signals from the Stock Market Valuation System are used. For the Market Momentum System, price trends from the FTSE 250 are used.

Strategy 5. Long-term FTSE 100 spread trading strategy

Long-term real annual return	Up to 32.2%
Long-term risk	3
Short-term risk	5
Effort	5

This strategy involves setting up an instant-access cash deposit fund and buying and selling quarterly FTSE 100 spread trades according to buy and sell signals from the Stock Market Valuation System. Stop-losses are set to exit trades when the price of a trade has fallen to a specified level and trades are also exited when prices have fallen to a level specified by the Market Momentum System. Profits or losses from trades are added to or subtracted from the instant-access cash deposit. The full strategy is described in a dedicated chapter.

Short-term risk is very high since spread trading involves gearing, which multiplies the percentage movements, up or down, of the FTSE 100. So, for a gearing multiple of 7, the trade would generate a loss of approximately 70% if the FTSE 100 price fell by 10%.

The long-term risk of this strategy is medium because the track record since the start of 1984 shows that over no five-year period would a loss in the fund value have been incurred.[2] In fact, most of the periods generated a significant profit.

I give the long-term real annual return as *up to 32.2%* because the actual return depends on the level of gearing chosen and the percentage stop-loss point chosen. I provide examples of the historic returns which you would have achieved at various levels of gearing and stop-loss. Most of these returns are outstanding. I also provide access to a simulator to test historic returns against your chosen gearing and stop-loss levels. At a compound annual real return of 32.2%, £1000 would grow in real terms to £4,334,000 over the course of 30 years.

The effort for running this strategy is relatively high, up to one hour per week, because positions need to be monitored daily and up to two trades need to be executed each quarter. Cash also needs to be switched, as needed, between the spread trading account and the instant-access cash account.

Strategy 6. Long-term FTSE 250 spread trading strategy

This is similar to the FTSE 100 spread trading strategy except that FTSE 250 spread trades are used instead of FTSE 100 spread trades. I have not constructed a long-term track record for this strategy because historic information on the buy and sell spreads for FTSE 250 spread trades is not available. The long-term return is likely to be higher than that for the FTSE 100 spread trading strategy, since the growth in the FTSE 250 price has been much higher than the growth in the FTSE 100 price. The gearing and stop-loss levels would have to be chosen very carefully because of the wide spreads on trade prices (at the time of writing there is a spread of about 0.6% between buy and sell prices). Short-term risk would probably be higher than that of the FTSE 100 spread trading strategy, with long-term risk about the same. The full strategy is described in a dedicated chapter.

---

2   For the example combinations of gearing and stop-loss levels which are provided.

Prospective future returns

As I will explain in the next chapter, the growth in the price of the FTSE 100 and FTSE 250 is closely tied to the growth rates of FTSE 100 and FTSE 250 dividends, respectively. Since 1984, the real compound annual growth of the FTSE 100 dividend has averaged 2.5%, but has been on a steadily declining trend. Over the last ten five-year periods (i.e. the five-year periods ending in January 2005 through to January 2014), the average real compound annual growth of the FTSE 100 dividend has been 0.7%. So I would expect future returns, over say the next ten years, to be lower than the average returns experienced over the last 30 years. After each strategy, I give my analysis of its prospective returns.

For Strategies 1 to 4, the prospective real annual returns, net of basic rate tax, range from 2.7% to 4.9%. I give the calculation of these returns in the chapters on each strategy. All of these returns are higher than the historical post-tax real return from cash of up to 1.2%. However, if governments globally maintain a policy of keeping interest rates artificially low, the prospective future real returns from cash will be even lower.

At the time of writing in September 2014, the best five-year, post-tax fixed rate return from a cash deposit provided a negative real return of -0.3%, using the prospective average inflation over the period of 2.7% annually. So, even taking into account the declining trend in FTSE 100 growth rates, it is highly likely that long-term investment returns from the FTSE 100 and FTSE 250 will continue to outstrip cash returns by a considerable margin. I have used the market expectations of average inflation over the next five years, as published by the Bank of England, to convert prospective actual returns into prospective real returns for all the strategies.

Throughout this book, when I refer to historic real returns from investments I have used the historic annual rate of inflation since 1984 of 3.58%.[3] When I refer to future returns from the strategies I have used the prospective future rate of inflation of 2.7%.

As regards the spread trading of Strategies 5 and 6, their prospective returns depend not just on the growth in the prices of the FTSE 100 and FTSE 250, but also on the volatility of those prices. Even though the growth rate of the FTSE 100 dividend has slowed in the last ten years, the value of a fund following the FTSE 100 spread trading strategy has increased considerably more in the last decade than in the decade prior to that. So, I would expect both of the spread

---

3   For FTSE 250 strategies, the historic annual inflation rate of 3.47% has been used, since this index started in 1986.

trading strategies to provide returns exceeding Strategies 1 to 4, at the expense of greatly increased short-term risk.

Note: The track records given for Strategies 2 to 6, which use FTSE 100 intrinsic valuations as signals to buy or sell, are based on ShareMaestro's FTSE 100 valuations, using default values of 10% for the risk premium and 2% for the real dividend growth rate (these terms will be explained later). The valuation spreadsheet included in this book provides FTSE 100 valuations which are very similar to those of ShareMaestro. Because the FTSE 100 real dividend growth rate has been on a declining trend since 1984, I recommend using a future real dividend growth rate for the FTSE 100 of 0% for current valuations. I also provide details of a web page where readers can find my latest estimate for the future long-term FTSE 100 real dividend growth rate.

CHAPTER 2. UK STOCK MARKET VALUATION SYSTEM

Plenty of people, especially fund managers, say that you cannot time the market. They think that trying to buy low and sell high is a fool's errand. Of course, fund managers have a vested interest in this assertion, because they want you to remain fully invested at all times. They do not earn commission when you are not invested.

It is certainly true that you cannot predict the precise peak and trough prices of the market. Anyone who claims they can is either an idiot or a liar. The peak and trough prices always reach extremes because of greed and panic, respectively. Trying to predict exactly how far greed or fear will stretch prices is impossible. However, it certainly *is* possible to buy the market when it is cheap and avoid it when it is dear.

In this chapter I will show you, step by step, how to create a spreadsheet to calculate the current intrinsic value of the market.

First, you need to understand my valuation principles for the FTSE 100. In *How to Value Shares and Outperform the Market* I explain the weaknesses of other methods used to value the FTSE 100, but here I will simply explain my valuation method (which is the method used in the strategies of this book).

The principles for valuing the FTSE 100

The sources of value

The overriding share valuation principle is that the current intrinsic value of a share depends on what is likely to happen in the future rather than what has happened in the past. Stock markets always look forward rather than backwards. Shares are valued on the basis of future prospects rather than on past performance. As stated by Simon Thompson in his book *Trading Secrets*, "The stock market is a forward-looking discounting mechanism."

When you invest in a share (or index), your return will normally come from only two sources, both of which are future events:

1. The price at which you sell.

2. Any dividends which you receive while holding the investment.

This means that any system to calculate the current value of a share must take account of these two fundamental factors.

In summary, my FTSE 100 valuation system:

- Calculates the future price of the FTSE 100 (in five years' time).

- Calculates the accumulated value of dividends and adds this to the future FTSE 100 price to determine the future value of the investment.

- Reduces the future investment value by a risk premium to compensate for the greater risk of holding a share rather than a virtually risk-free gilt.

- Discounts the risk-adjusted future investment value back to today's value by using, as a discount rate, the annual return on five-year gilts (held to redemption). The actual yields on gilts vary according to the gains or losses which will be made on redemption of the gilt. This gives the current intrinsic value of the FTSE 100.

- Compares the above intrinsic value with the current market price to establish if the price represents good, bad or fair value. The ratio of current value is expressed as a percentage. Over 100% indicates that the value is greater than the price, and below 100% indicates that the value is lower than the price.

Measuring value effectively

To be effective a FTSE 100 valuation system must have three important features:

1. The calculation of the FTSE 100's intrinsic value always involves a certain amount of judgement. The best valuation methodology *will minimise the amount of judgement required.*

2. A share valuation will only be valid for a snapshot in time. Any changes to the factors which underpin the valuation will change the valuation itself. It is therefore vital that any valuation system should allow the investor to *assess the impact of potential changes in the factor values on the resulting valuation.* This facility is known as sensitivity analysis or scenario testing. It is a key feature of my system.

3. It is also vital that a share valuation system *takes into account the economic environment* – by which I mean the current and prospective levels of inflation, interest rates and economic growth. Economic growth is the total increase in the value of goods and services produced by an economy (in our case the UK). Economic growth is normally measured in real (i.e. inflation-adjusted) terms and is represented in my valuation system as sustainable real dividend growth. A valuation system which does not take into account the economic environment is meaningless as it would be ignoring the real world.

As far as I know, my system is the only FTSE 100 valuation system which incorporates all three of these key features.

A five-year investment period

My system calculates the future value of a share or index in five years' time. It uses a five-year investment period to allow growth companies to grow and bubbles to burst. This period has proved consistently successful for valuing the FTSE 100 and its constituent shares. It is true that many fund managers have a *churn rate* which is much less than five years – often as little as six months. However, the most successful value investing fund managers, such as Neil Woodford and Terry Smith, have an average share holding period of more than five years. Five years is also the typical holding period for structured equity products and for National Savings Certificates.

Dividends at the heart of the process

You can also see from the summary above that my valuation system uses the dividend as the heart of the valuation process. There are several reasons for this:

- Dividends, unlike earnings, cannot be fiddled. They have to be paid out of hard cash. A sure sign that a company is in trouble is if it reduces or even cancels its dividend or forces shareholders to accept extra shares instead of the dividend. For example, on 22 April 2008, RBS announced a decision to pay its interim dividend in shares rather than in cash. Subsequently, the dire condition of the company became apparent and the share price fell by more than 90%.

- Reinvested dividends form between 80% and 90% of the total return for a long-term value investor.

- The level of actual and expected dividends has a profound effect on a share or market price. The FTSE 100 nosedived after the big banks cancelled their dividends in reaction to the credit crunch mayhem of 2008. Banks formed a significant proportion of the overall FTSE 100 dividend. Similarly, in

17

2010, the BP share price more than halved when the company suspended its dividend in response to the Gulf of Mexico oil spill disaster. The share price only began to recover when it became clear that the company was considering reinstating the dividend, albeit at a lower level.

The detailed steps to determine current value

The detailed steps which my system uses to determine the current FTSE 100 value are as follows (I will explain these steps in full later):

1. Calculate the current FTSE 100 dividend.

2. Calculate the compound prospective five-year actual growth rate of this dividend by combining the expected real dividend growth rate with the projected average inflation rate for the five-year period.

3. Calculate the projected dividend for the final year by applying the above actual growth rate for five years to the current dividend.

4. Calculate the FTSE 100 dividend yield for the final year by applying a system-specific formula to the projected inflation rate for the end of the fifth year (dividend yields are influenced by the contemporaneous inflation rate).

5. Calculate the projected end-period FTSE 100 price by applying the above projected final year dividend to the above projected end-period dividend yield.

6. Calculate the projected end-period investment value by adding the value of projected dividends reinvested over the five-year period to the projected FTSE 100 price.

7. Discount the above investment value by the risk premium. I provide the risk premium to use for the FTSE 100.

8. Discount the above future value back to today's value by using, as a discount rate, the gross redemption yield on five-year gilts. I explain how discounting works later in this chapter.

9. Finally, express the resulting value as a percentage of today's market price. A percentage valuation below 100 indicates poor value and a percentage valuation above 100 indicates good value.

Don't worry if all this looks too complicated. I will take you through, step-by-step, how to set up a spreadsheet to do all the calculations. All you will have to do, when you have set up the master spreadsheet, is input a few pieces of data to get further FTSE 100 valuations. After that, it should take no more than ten minutes to get an up-to-date valuation.

Creating a spreadsheet to value the FTSE 100

The valuation system created by the spreadsheet has a proven track record, which I will explain later in this chapter. The valuations are very close to those produced by ShareMaestro. The system forms the core of four out of the seven investment strategies covered in this book. I will give step-by-step instructions on how to create this spreadsheet.

I will detail:

- Each input field and where to find the source data.
- Each result and calculation field and the associated formulae.
- The cell references for each field.

You will need access to the internet. I suggest that you bookmark the source URLs which I provide for ease of access in the future.

If you do not want to build the spreadsheet or update the input data whenever you need an updated valuation of the FTSE 100, you can subscribe to ShareMaestro. This service sends clients a weekly spreadsheet giving valuations of the FTSE 100 and of shares in the FTSE All-Share index (www.sharemaestro. co.uk).

I will give the formulae in Microsoft Excel notation as this is by far the most prevalent spreadsheet software in use. You will need to insert the equivalent formulae for any other spreadsheet, or you could splash out about £50 and buy Excel. Cell references are simple: Cell B6 means the cell in column B, row 6.

I will be using Excel in a basic form. Excel can be used in some very sophisticated ways and is heavily employed within the equity divisions of investment banks. If you have not got a clue about how spreadsheets work, there are plenty of books specifically on Excel (e.g. *Excel 2010 for Dummies*). There are also very good free online courses from Microsoft. You will often be directed to these if you use the Help button within the Excel software, or you can find them on the Microsoft website (office.microsoft.com/en-us/excel-help).

Setting up the spreadsheet template

First, you need to set up a spreadsheet template, with labels in the appropriate cells, as shown in figure 1. This template will be used to accept input values and results formulae. It is important that you follow the template structure exactly.

If you are using Microsoft Excel, ensure that the Analysis Toolpak add-in is activated. You can tell if this add-in has been activated, or if you still need to set it up, by looking at the result in cell D24 when you have created the spreadsheet below. If cell D24 shows an error, rather than a numerical value, then you will need to activate the Analysis Toolpak. Use the Help function in Excel to find out how to do this, as the method varies according to the version of Excel which you have. You can also find help online from the Excel help pages on the Microsoft website (office.microsoft.com/en-us/excel-help).

Set column widths as follows:

Column	Width
A	30
B	10
C	30
D	12

Except for date fields in B6, B23 and B24, you should set the format for each data cell in columns B and D to 'number' and set the number of decimal places for displaying each number to 1 or 2. Cell D7 should be set to 3 decimal places.

FIGURE 1. TEMPLATE FOR THE FTSE 100 VALUATION

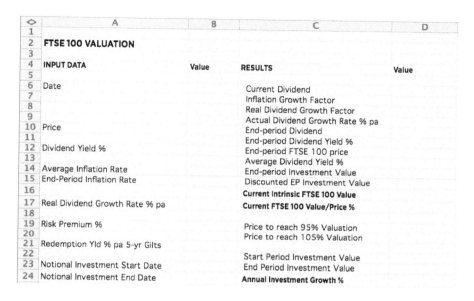

You can download this template spreadsheet from the Harriman House website (harriman-house.com/files/StockMarketValuationSystem_spreadsheet.xls).

Inputting data into the template

You only need seven items of data to produce a current intrinsic valuation of the FTSE 100. Five of these items are factual and two are judgemental. I will guide you on how to determine the values for the judgemental data.

I will use as an example the data for 3 March 2009, which is the lowest price the FTSE 100 reached after the 2007/8 credit crunch. This will also allow you to verify that you have set up the spreadsheet correctly by comparing your results with those in this section.

You should input the following data in the appropriate cells, as described below.

Cell B6: Date

Enter the date for which you are making the valuation. This is a date label and is not used in the spreadsheet calculations.

Entry in B6: 03-Mar-09

Cell B10: Price

You can obtain the price of the FTSE 100 from the *Financial Times* website (markets.ft.com/research/Markets/Data-Archive).

Scroll down to 'Download reports' and, in the drop-down menus, select:

- **Category**: Equities
- **Report**: FTSE Actuaries Share Indices – UK Series
- **Date**: Select the date of your choice (in this case 3 March 2009), click on the 'download' button and the report should appear in PDF format. In practice, the available *FT* data only covers the last four years, but it is unlikely that you will need to do retrospective valuations further back than this. The purpose of this worked example is to get you accustomed to the data sources and it does not matter that you cannot access the figures for 2009. Simply enter the value given below into your spreadsheet. If you want to verify that you are picking up the right data from the sources, you can cross-check the input values given in figure 8 on page 46 for the FTSE 100 valuation of 17 October 2014.

On the report the FTSE 100 data is in the first row, with the current price shown in the second column under the date.

If this service is not available, on the same page click on the 'Download PDF' button to the right of 'World Markets at a glance'. Navigate the downloaded PDF until you find a block headed 'FTSE ACTUARIES SHARE INDICES'. The latest FTSE 100 price is shown in the first column of the first line. You will probably need to use the zoom button to read it.

The current FTSE 100 price can also be found widely on the internet – just make a search for 'FTSE 100 price' – or in broadsheet newspapers.

Entry in B10: 3512.1

Cell B12: Dividend Yield %

To obtain the dividend yield use the *Financial Times* report downloaded above for Price.

The FTSE 100 dividend yield is shown under the column headed Div. yld%.

The current FTSE 100 dividend yield is also available from broadsheet newspapers.

Entry in B12: 5.95

Cell B14: Average Inflation Rate

You can obtain the average inflation rate from the Bank of England website (www.bankofengland.co.uk/statistics/yieldcurve/index.htm).

The Bank of England produces a daily report to show the market's inflation expectations as implied by the prices of market instruments. Scroll down to the section headed 'Implied Inflation (government liability)' against an Excel icon.

Click on this wording and a dialogue box will appear. Click on OK to open the file (normally with Microsoft Excel). The file should download to your computer. If it does not open automatically, browse to your downloads folder and open the spreadsheet.

Click on the 'spot curve' tab and scroll sideways to the column headed 5.00. This shows the average inflation expected over the next five years. Read across from the required date on the left (normally the last date if you are doing a current valuation) to get the appropriate figure under the column headed 5.00.

Normally there is a time-lag of one working day in this data being updated. Don't worry if you have to use the previous day's figure as there is normally very little change in the figure over one day.

I do not advise using my System if the average inflation rate is over 10.5%. In the case of this example, for 3 March 2009 the figure shown was 1.5%.

Entry in B14: 1.50

Cell B15: End-Period Inflation Rate

Using the Excel spreadsheet just downloaded from the Bank of England, click on the 'fwd curve' tab and scroll sideways to the column headed 5.00. This shows the inflation rate expected at the end of the next five years. Read across from the required date on the left (normally the last date if you are doing a current valuation) to get the appropriate figure under the column headed 5.00.

Normally there is a time-lag of one working day in this data being updated. Don't worry if you have to use the previous day's figure as there is normally very little change in the figure over one day.

I do not advise using my System if the end-period inflation rate is negative or over 10.5%. In our example, for 3 March 2009 the figure shown in the spreadsheet is 3.25%.

Entry in B15: 3.25

Cell B17: Real Dividend Growth Rate %pa

The expected real dividend growth rate is a critical element in determining the FTSE 100 valuation. It is the real compound annual percentage growth rate expected in the FTSE 100 dividend over the next five years. There is no source for this, it is assessed by judgement. The real growth rate is the growth in excess of inflation.

Since 1986, the first year when a reliable FTSE 100 dividend yield is available, the compound real FTSE 100 five-year growth rate has ranged between -3.05% and +7.5%. The long-term annual real growth rate has averaged +2.5%. However, the rate has trended downwards, as is clear from table 2.

TABLE 2: COMPOUND ANNUAL FIVE-YEAR REAL DIVIDEND GROWTH RATE FOR THE YEARS ENDING 31 DECEMBER

Period	% average real growth rate
1990-1997	4.2
1998-2005	0.8
2006-2013	0.5

The actual (including inflation) FTSE 100 dividend has grown over every five-year period since 1984, although sometimes by a very small amount.

HOW TO DETERMINE WHAT REAL DIVIDEND GROWTH RATE TO USE

In view of the downward trend, and in the absence of any more convincing information, I would now use 0% p.a. as the default real dividend growth rate for the FTSE 100. Sometimes there may be strong reasons for deviating from this default. You can find the latest forecast for the five-year compound annual FTSE 100 dividend growth rate on the ShareMaestro website (www.sharemaestro.co.uk/FTSE100dividend.shtml).

A HISTORY LESSON

- In *How to Value Shares and Outperform the Market* I used the same date of 3 March 2009 as an example of how to value the FTSE 100. As I wrote that book in 2011, we did not then know what the actual five-year real dividend growth rate was going to be. The UK was in the grip of the most severe recession since the second world war and the consensus amongst analysts was that dividends would be cut by 30% over the coming year. So I calculated the real prospective compound annual dividend growth rate to be -6.0%.

- In retrospect this assumption was unduly pessimistic, as -6.0% was double the worst ever five-year real growth rate experienced previously. Although the FTSE 100 dividend did fall in real terms for the first two years, it recovered strongly thereafter. The actual rate turned out to be -0.9%.

- Nevertheless, the direction of the valuation proved to be absolutely correct. The valuation showed the FTSE 100 to be worth 43% more than its market price – a very strong buy signal. Over the next five years the FTSE 100 price soared by 91%.

Entry in B17: 0.00

Cell B19: Risk Premium %

The risk premium compensates for the greater risk of holding equities than of holding a virtually risk-free gilt (if held to redemption). In my System, the end period investment value is risk-adjusted as follows:

(end-period investment value x 100)/(100 + risk premium)

This is a somewhat different method from most risk premium models, which use an annual discount rate to cater for the risk premium.

There is no source for the risk premium, as it is a matter of judgement and experience. However, back-testing my System for every trading day to the start of the FTSE 100 suggests that 10% is an appropriate figure for the FTSE 100 over a five-year period.

Entry in B19: 10.00

Cell B21: Redemption Yld % pa 5-year Gilts

You can obtain the redemption yield per year for five-year gilts from the *Financial Times* website (markets.ft.com/research/Markets/Data-Archive).

Scroll down to 'Download reports' and, in the drop-down menus, select:

- **Category**: Bonds & Rates
- **Report**: FTSE UK Gilts Indices

- **Date**: Select the date of your choice (in this case 3 March 2009) and click on the 'download' button and the report should appear in PDF format. Once again, in practice the *FT* data only goes back four years, so you will not be able to access the report for 3 March 2009. Simply enter the value given below into your spreadsheet – the important thing for now is to get used to the data sources used in the Valuation System. See also the comments under cell B10 above.

In the middle of the page, there are three rows under the heading Yield indices. Select the first row '5 yrs' and the value for the appropriate date. This is the compound risk-free rate for a gilt held for five years to redemption. For this example, the figure shown is 2.41, so we enter this in B21.

If this service is not available, on the same page click on the 'Download PDF' button to the right of 'FTSE 500, Fixed Incomes, Commodities, Interest rates'. Navigate the downloaded PDF until you find a block headed 'GILTS: UK FTSE ACTUARIES INDICES'. Find the rows headed 'Yield Indices'. The latest 5 year gilt redemption yield is shown in the first of these rows in the first column. You will probably need to use the zoom button to read it.

You can also obtain a value for this entry from UK broadsheet newspapers, which list the prices and yields for a selection of gilts. Choose a non-index-linked gilt with a redemption date approximately five years away from the current date and select the quoted redemption yield (often abbreviated to 'Rm').

Entry in B21: 2.41

Cell B23: Notional Investment Start Date

In conjunction with the next cell, B24, this is used by Excel to calculate the five-year annual compound investment growth rates. It does not matter which two dates are used as long as they are exactly five years apart. Ensure that both cells are formatted to accept dates. I suggest using the dd/mm/yyyy format.

Entry in B23: 01/01/2000

Cell B24: Notional Investment End Date

Entry in B24: 01/01/2005

Inputting formulae into the template to get results

These formulae will all be in column D. Each formula starts with an equals sign (=), which must be keyed into the cell at the beginning of each formula and it must be directly followed by the formula without a space between it and the equals sign. After inputting each formula, you should check that the result shown in your spreadsheet is the same as given below. If it is not, the formula will not have been entered correctly.

Cell D6: Current Dividend

This is the current dividend of the FTSE 100, net of the tax credit. The dividend yield of the FTSE 100 is calculated from the dividends of the 100 constituent companies, weighted by the market capitalisation of the companies. You calculate the current net dividend of the FTSE 100 in the same way that you would calculate the net dividend of a share. Multiply the current percentage dividend yield of the FTSE 100 (B10) by the current market price of the FTSE 100 (B12).

Formula entry in D6: =(B10*B12)/100

Result: 209.0

Cell D7: Inflation Growth Factor

This is the multiplier to apply in order to increase a number by the average inflation rate (in B14) for one year.

Formula Entry in D7: =(1+(B14/100))

Result: 1.015

Cell D8: Real Dividend Growth Factor

This is the multiplier to apply the real dividend growth rate (in B17) to the current dividend for one year. It is used in conjunction with the Inflation Growth Factor to produce the projected annual actual dividend growth rate, as shown in cell D9.

Formula Entry in D8: =(1+(B17/100))

Result: 1.00

Cell D9: Actual Dividend Growth % p.a.

This is calculated by combining the real dividend growth rate (cell B17) with the average inflation rate (cell B9). This annual growth rate is compounded on the current dividend for five years to project the end-period FTSE 100 dividend, as shown in cell D10.

Formula entry in D9: =((D7*D8)-1)*100

Result: 1.50

Cell D10: End-period Dividend

This is the projected dividend in the fifth year of the period, calculated by compounding the current net dividend (D6) by the actual dividend growth rate (D9) for five successive years. The symbol ^ multiplies the amount before the ^ by itself the number of times given by the number after the ^. This is called compounding. Hence, the amount in brackets is compounded five times.

Formula entry in D10: =D6*(1+(D9/100))^5

Result: 225.1

Cell D11: End-period Dividend Yield %

This is the projected FTSE 100 dividend yield percentage at the end of the five-year period. It takes into account the projected inflation rate for the end of the period (cell B15). The calculations for this yield in ShareMaestro are proprietary and complex. The following formula comes very close to the ShareMaestro value and uses the projected end-period inflation rate in cell B15. The final figure in the formula, in a range from 1.8 to 2.5, should be chosen as follows:

End period Inflation Rate %	Final figure in formula
0 to 4.9	2.5
5.0 to 6.0	2.3
6.1 to 6.8	2.1
6.9 to 9.0	2.0
9.1 to 10.5	1.8

The final figure used in the formula below is 2.5 as the End-period Inflation Rate in B15 is 3.25.

Formula entry in D11: =((B15/10.5)*3)+2.5

Result: 3.43

Please note that this spreadsheet cannot be used when the projected end-period inflation rate is either negative or more than 10.5%. At the time of writing, neither of these values has occurred since the launch of the FTSE 100 index.

Cell D12: End-period FTSE 100 price

This price follows directly from the end-period dividend (cell D10) and the end-period dividend yield (cell D11). It is calculated as follows:

Formula entry in D12: =(100/D11)*D10

Result: 6566

Cell D13: Average Dividend Yield %

This is calculated from the average of the current dividend yield (B12) and the end-period dividend yield (B11):

Formula entry in D13: =(B12+D11)/2

Result: 4.69

Cell D14: End-Period Investment Value

This is the end-period investment value, assuming basic rate UK income tax is paid on the dividends. It is calculated by adding to the end-period FTSE 100 price (B12) five years' worth of the average dividend, net of UK basic rate tax (i.e. the net dividend paid by the company). Every time you reinvest a dividend, you increase your percentage holding in the company by the percentage dividend yield.

So, if the dividend yield were 3.5%, you would increase your holding in the company by 3.5% through reinvesting the dividend. That is why the end-period FTSE 100 price is used as the base on which to calculate the uplift in value through dividend reinvestment.

In order to understand why the End-period FTSE 100 price is used in this formula, imagine you bought 3512 shares at £1 each in the FTSE 100. The projected End-period FTSE 100 price has been calculated in D12 to be 6566 and Average Dividend Yield in D13 as 4.69%. On that basis your investment, including reinvesting dividends in the FTSE 100, if held for five years would play out as follows:

End of year	FTSE 100 price	Share price £	Avg div @ 4.69%	Extra shares bought	No. of shares held at year end	Nominal value of shares held at year end
Start	3512	1.00	0	0	3512	3512
1	3980	1.13	187	165	3677	4167
2	4511	1.28	221	172	3849	4944
3	5112	1.46	263	181	4030	5866
4	5794	1.65	312	189	4219	6959
5	6566	1.87	370	198	4417	8257

The second column shows the FTSE 100 growing progressively at 13.33% pa for five years to go from 3512 (B10) to 6566 (D12). That means each original £1 share would grow as in the third column. At the end of year 1, a dividend of 4.69% of 3980 = £187 would be received. You want to reinvest that but now shares are £1.13 each so you buy 165 more shares and your holding grows to 3677 shares.

At the end of year 2, again a dividend of 4.69% is paid but you now have 3677 shares each worth £1.28 so it is now 4.69% of 3677 x 1.28 = £221 which you use to buy 172 more shares at £1.28. Your holding for the third year goes up to 3849 shares.

This continues to the end of year 5, by which time the holding is worth 8257, which is the result in D14. For those mathematically minded, Price (B10) would appear in both the nominator and denominator of the full formula to calculate this and so drops out.

Formula entry in D14: =D12*((1+(D13/100))^5)

Result: 8257

This formula would need to be amended if a change to UK tax rules meant that basic rate tax had to be paid on the dividend received from the company. Currently a basic rate UK taxpayer receives the dividend paid by the company and does not need to pay any further UK tax on it.

Cell D15: Discounted EP Investment Value

This value is calculated by discounting the projected end-period (EP) investment value shown in cell D14 back to today's value by using, as a discount rate, the gross annual yield on five-year gilts held to redemption (B21). Discounting is the opposite of compounding. Compounding takes a present value and increases it by an annual interest rate for x number of years to get a future value. Discounting takes a future value and reduces it by an annual interest rate for a number of years to get a present value. So the present value of the investment will always be less than the future value (unless we get negative gilt rates!).

Formula entry in D15: =D14*((100/(100+B21))^5)

Result: 7330

Cell D16: Current Intrinsic FTSE 100 Value

This is the present discounted end-period investment value (D15), further discounted by the risk premium (B19). This is the current intrinsic value of the FTSE 100 calculated by the Stock Market Valuation System from all the input values.

Formula entry in D16: =D15*(100/(100+B19))

Result: 6664

Cell D17: Current FTSE 100 Value/Price %

This expresses the current FTSE 100 intrinsic value (D16) as a percentage of the current FTSE 100 market price (B10):

Formula entry in D17: =(D16/B10)*100

Result: 190

Cell D19: Price to reach 95% valuation

The purpose of this cell and the next is to show the price the FTSE 100 would have to reach for certain buy (D20) and sell (D19) trigger points used by strategies which we will discuss later. I recommend that, if you are following Strategies 3 to 6, you undertake weekly FTSE 100 valuations. These cells save you having to perform daily valuations, assuming that the only significant changes in input values between each week are likely to be the FTSE 100 price and the associated dividend yield.

Formula entry in D19: =(B10*D17)/95

Result: 7014

Cell D20: Price to reach 105% Valuation

Formula entry in D20: =(B10*D17)/105

Result: 6346

Cell D22: Start Period Investment Value

This is the price of the FTSE 100 at the date of the valuation, expressed as a negative to comply with Excel's formula for calculating compound growth rates.

Formula entry in D22: =-B10

Result: -3512

Cell D23: End Period Investment Value

This is the projected investment value in five years' time, including reinvested dividends but before any discount for the gilt yield or risk premium (D14).

Formula entry in D23: =D14

Result: 8257

Cell D24: Annual Investment Growth %

This is the projected compound annual investment growth from the start-period investment value to the end-period investment value. The formula uses the Excel formula for calculating compound growth rates. The 0.1 inside the brackets is an estimate of the result (equivalent to 10%), to assist Excel in performing the calculation.

Formula entry in D24: =XIRR(D22:D23,B23:B24,0.1)*100

Result: 18.6

You have now completed the construction of the spreadsheet and you should double-check that your results are the same as in figure 2. If not, one or more of the formulae has been entered incorrectly.

FIGURE 2. RESULTS OF THE FTSE 100 VALUATION

◇	A	B	C	D
1				
2	**FTSE 100 VALUATION**			
3				
4	**INPUT DATA**	**Value**	**RESULTS**	**Value**
5				
6	Date	03-Mar-09	Current Dividend	209.0
7			Inflation Growth Factor	1.015
8			Real Dividend Growth Factor	1.00
9			Actual Dividend Growth Rate % pa	1.50
10	Price	3512.1	End-period Dividend	225.1
11			End-period Dividend Yield %	3.43
12	Dividend Yield %	5.95	End-period FTSE 100 price	6566
13			Average Dividend Yield %	4.69
14	Average Inflation Rate	1.50	End-period Investment Value	8257
15	End-Period Inflation Rate	3.25	Discounted EP Investment Value	7330
16			**Current Intrinsic FTSE 100 Value**	**6664**
17	Real Dividend Growth Rate % pa	0.00	**Current FTSE 100 Value/Price %**	**190**
18				
19	Risk Premium %	10.00	Price to reach 95% Valuation	7014
20			Price to reach 105% Valuation	6346
21	Redemption Yld % pa 5-yr Gilts	2.41		
22			Start Period Investment Value	-3512
23	Notional Investment Start Date	01/01/2000	End Period Investment Value	8257
24	Notional Investment End Date	01/01/2005	**Annual Investment Growth %**	**18.6**

Having ensured that all the formulae have been entered correctly and that the results equate to those in figure 2, you should create a master spreadsheet which can be used for future valuations. Clear all the input values in cells B6 to B22 and save this sheet with your own choice of file name. The values in cells B23 and B24 do not need to be removed as it does not matter which dates are used providing they are exactly five years apart.

Extending the spreadsheet to personalise investment growth

If you only want to use the spreadsheet to generate percentage valuations for the FTSE 100, in order to use them as buy and sell triggers for the strategies we discuss later, this spreadsheet extension is not necessary.

However, if you plan to use the projected annual investment growth figures in cell D24 to make investment decisions, and you are a higher rate taxpayer or are liable to pay capital gains tax on any realised profits, this extension is essential, as it calculates your projected post-tax investment returns.

You can also factor your own personal risk premium into the calculation of returns. The investment growth figure shown in cell D24 only applies to basic rate taxpayers, who will not pay any capital gains tax on profits realised from the investment.

You should first add extra fields to the template underneath the existing valuation template, as shown in figure 3.

FIGURE 3. BLANK TEMPLATE FOR PERSONALISED INVESTMENT GROWTH

◇	A	B	C	D
26	**PERSONAL PROJECTED POST-TAX ANNUAL INVESTMENT GROWTH**			
27	Key: PIV = End-period Personal Investment Value, PRP = Personal Risk Premium HR = Higher Rate			
28				
29	Personal extra HR tax on divs		PIV post HR tax on dividends	
30	Personal Risk Premium		PIV post HR tax and PRP	
31	Personal CGT %		End-period FTSE 100 price post PRP	
32			Capital Gain ex reinvested dividends	
33			CGT on gain ex dividend reinvestment	
34			Net divs received post HR tax	
35			% Capital Gains ex reinvested divs	
36			Estimated Capital Gain on divs	
37			Estimated CGT on divs	
38			Total CGT payable	
39			Start period investment value	
40			PIV ex HR tax, CGT and PRP	
41			**Annual Personal Investment Grth**	

Inputting data

Cell B29: Personal extra HR tax on divs

This is the percentage of extra tax which higher rate (HR) taxpayers have to pay on the net dividend. The net dividend will have had 10% tax deducted (hence 'net') prior to the dividend being paid to you. If you are a basic rate taxpayer you do not have to pay any additional tax on the dividend. However, higher rate taxpayers have to pay additional tax on the net dividend.

The first tier of UK higher rate tax is 40% at the time of writing. HR taxpayers have to pay 32.5% tax on the gross dividend, i.e. the dividend before the 10% is deducted, but they do get credited with having paid the 10%. This is equivalent to HR taxpayers having to pay an extra 25% tax on the net dividend. (This is calculated as follows: say the gross dividend in question is £100, so less the 10% automatically deducted, this gives £90 net. HR taxpayers need to pay 32.5% tax in total on the £100, which is £32.50. They are credited with having paid £10 already, so they must pay a further £22.50 from the remaining £90. This is an extra tax of 25% on the £90.)

Those who pay the *additional rate* of tax at 45% will have to pay 37.5% tax on the gross dividend, but they do get credited with having paid the 10%. This is equivalent to an extra 30.55% on the net dividend received.

Obviously, if these rates change, your input values would have to change correspondingly. Also please note that no extra higher rate tax would be applicable for investments held in a tax-free wrapper such as an ISA or a SIPP.

For the sake of this example, we will assume a 40% higher rate taxpayer.

Entry in B29: 25

Cell B30: Personal Risk Premium

The default risk premium of 10% (B19) is only taken into account in the current FTSE 100 intrinsic value calculation (D16). It is not taken into account in the investment growth calculation (D24), which uses the projected end-period investment value (D14).

If you want a safety margin, because you believe that equities are riskier than for example cash, enter your chosen percentage personal risk premium (PRP) here as the figure in B19 will not be used in the calculations below. The chosen personal risk premium will reduce projected investment values by 100/(100 +PRP).

Entry in B30: 10

Cell B31: Personal CGT %

This is your marginal capital gains tax rate, after the annual capital gains tax allowance has been used up. Currently the rates are 18% for basic rate taxpayers and 28% for higher rate taxpayers. Again, please note that no extra higher rate tax would be applicable for investments held in a tax-free wrapper such as an ISA or a SIPP.

Entry in B31: 28

Inputting formulae into the template to get results

As before, you should check that, after inputting each formula, your result corresponds with the result given. If not, there is a mistake in the formula entry.

Cell D29: PIV post HR tax on dividends

PIV is the Personal Investment Value. This is the end period investment value but now taking into account the need to pay higher rate tax on the dividends prior to reinvesting them, which will reduce the end period investment value. The formula is essentially the same as that used for calculating the end-period investment value in D14, except for the inclusion of the personal extra HR tax on dividends (B29). As B29 is a percentage it has to be deducted from 100 and then divided by 10,000 to turn it into a decimal, before multiplying the average dividend yield (D13) by it.

Formula entry in D29: =D12*(1+D13*((100-B29)/10000))^5

Result: 7805

Cell D30: PIV post HR tax and PRP

This reduces the value in cell D29 by any personal risk premium (PRP) chosen in B30.

Formula entry in D30: =(D29*100)/(100+B30)

Result: 7095

Cell D31: End-period FTSE 100 price post PRP

This is the projected end-period FTSE 100 price (D12) reduced by any personal risk premium in B30.

Formula entry in D31: =(D12*100)/(100+B30)

Result: 5969

Cell D32: Capital Gain ex reinvested dividends

The projected capital gain on the original investment is the end-period FTSE 100 price after adjusting for the PRP from D31, less the initial FTSE 100 price (B10) at the valuation date in B6. However, this does not include the capital gain arising from extra investment as a result of reinvested dividends, which is calculated in D36.

Formula entry in D32: =D31-B10

Result: 2457

Cell D33: CGT on gain ex dividend reinvestment

This is the capital gains tax payable at your personal capital gains tax rate (B31) on any gain that arises. The formula prevents a negative tax being charged on any loss. If there has been no gain, i.e. D32 is zero or negative, then this formula will give a value for D33 of zero. Please note the comma after 100 in the formula.

Formula entry in D33: =IF(D32>0,D32*B31/100,0)

Result: 688

Cell D34: Net divs received post HR tax

These are the dividends, net of tax, including HR tax if applicable, received during the five-year investment period (with D30 having taken into account any personal risk premium in B30).

Formula entry in D34: =D30-D31

Result: 1126

Cell D35: % Capital Gains ex reinvested divs

This is the capital gain from D32, expressed as a percentage of the initial investment (B10), excluding reinvested dividends.

Formula entry in D35: =(D32/B10)*100

Result: 70

Cell D36: Estimated Capital Gain on divs

This is the estimated capital gain arising from dividend reinvestment. The formula first checks that the percentage gain from the investment excluding reinvested dividends (D35) is positive and, if it is, applies half of that percentage gain to the total of net dividends received (D35), because on average the dividends will have been invested for half the time of the original investment.

It is therefore assumed that the average percentage capital gain on reinvested dividends will be half the percentage gain on the original investment. Please note the comma before the zero at the end of the formula. If D35 is not positive, the formula gives the result of zero.

Formula entry in D36: =IF(D35>0,(D34*D35)/(100*2),0)

Result: 394

Cell D37: Estimated CGT on divs

This is the estimated capital gains tax payable at your personal capital gains tax rate on dividends (B31).

Formula entry in D37: =(D36*B31)/100

Result: 110

Cell D38: Total CGT payable

This is the total CGT payable on the initial investment and on reinvested dividends.

Formula entry in D38: =D33+D37

Result: 798

Cell D39: Start period investment value

This is the initial investment value (FTSE 100 price in B10), expressed as a negative to comply with the Excel compound growth rate formula to show that this is an outflow.

Formula entry in D39: =-B10

Result: -3512

Cell D40: PIV ex HR tax, CGT and PRP

This is the end-period personal investment value reduced, if applicable, by higher rate tax on dividends, capital gains tax and any personal risk premium.

Formula entry in D40: =D30-D38

Result: 6297

Cell D41: Annual Personal Investment Grth

This is the compound annual percentage growth of the FTSE 100 investment over the five-year period, taking into account your personal risk premium and tax circumstances. It assumes that you sell the investment after five years and therefore trigger potential capital gains tax. The 0.1 in the formula, which is equivalent to 10%, is an estimate to help Excel determine the answer.

Formula entry in D41: =XIRR(D39:D40,B23:B24,0.1)*100

Result: 12.4

In this example, the application of a personal risk premium of 10%, CGT at 28% and extra higher rate tax on dividends of 25% has reduced the projected annual investment growth rate from the original 18.6% in figure 2 to 12.4%.

When you have finished entering the input data and the formulae, your spreadsheet should look like that shown in figure 4.

FIGURE 4. RESULTS FOR PERSONAL PROJECTED POST-TAX INVESTMENT GROWTH

◇	A	B	C	D
26	**PERSONAL PROJECTED POST-TAX ANNUAL INVESTMENT GROWTH**			
27	Key: PIV = End-period Personal Investment Value, PRP = Personal Risk Premium HR = Higher Rate			
28				
29	Personal extra HR tax on divs	25	PIV post HR tax on dividends	7805
30	Personal Risk Premium	10	PIV post HR tax and PRP	7095
31	Personal CGT %	28	End-period FTSE 100 price post PRP	5969
32			Capital Gain ex reinvested dividends	2457
33			CGT on gain ex dividend reinvestment	688
34			Net divs received post HR tax	1126
35			% Capital Gains ex reinvested divs	70
36			Estimated Capital Gain on divs	394
37			Estimated CGT on divs	110
38			Total CGT payable	798
39			Start period investment value	-3512
40			PIV ex HR tax, CGT and PRP	6297
41			**Annual Personal Investment Grth**	**12.4**

The two main uses of FTSE 100 valuations

There are two main uses of the FTSE 100 valuations:

1. To use the percentage valuations as buy and sell triggers for the investment strategies described in this book. As we will see, these buy and sell triggers work for the FTSE 250 index as well as for the FTSE 100.

2. To compare the projected five-year FTSE 100 investment returns with other investment options such as fixed-rate cash deposits. This second use does not apply to the FTSE 250 since the returns for the FTSE 250 will be different from the FTSE 100 (generally higher because the FTSE 250 dividend growth tends to be higher than that of the FTSE 100).

1. When to buy and sell

The percentage valuations of the Market Valuation System can be used as buy and sell triggers. The higher the percentage valuation above 100%, the stronger is the buy signal. Conversely, the lower the percentage valuation below 100%, the stronger is the sell signal.

However, if you wait for extreme valuations, there will be very few buy and sell signals. On the other hand, if you buy and sell at valuations very close to 100%, you will generate frequent trades, some of which will prove to be unsuccessful. Analysis of the FTSE 100 dynamics shows that, for this System, a consistently reliable buy/sell spread is 105%/95%. In other words, you buy the FTSE 100 when the valuation reaches at least 105% and sell when the valuation falls to 95% or below.

Table 3 shows the results of using this buy/sell spread since the inception of the FTSE 100 in 1984. The results are striking:

- Every single purchase made a capital gain on the subsequent sale.

- Capital losses occurred during four of the six out-of-market periods. By being out of the market you would have been shielded from these losses.

- Total capital gains during the in-market periods were 5766.

- The out-of-market periods suffered a total net capital loss of 380.

This is a clear, long-term validation of the Valuation System.

Notes

- These valuations use the default risk premium of 10% and the long-term real dividend growth rate of 2% and are those produced by ShareMaestro.

- FTSE 100 investment did not start until 1985 because the FTSE 100 valuation was below 105% before this.

- The price at 30 September 2014 is a hold rather than a sale since a sell signal had not yet occurred following the previous purchase.

TABLE 3. TRACK RECORD OF MARKET VALUATION SYSTEM BUY AND SELL SIGNALS, USING THE 105%/95% BUY/SELL SPREAD

In the market

Buy date	Buy price	Sell date	Sell price	Price gain
26/06/1985	1237	21/11/1985	1443	207
28/10/1987	1658	11/07/1989	2251	593
09/04/1990	2228	24/12/1993	3412	1185
07/03/1995	2977	12/10/1995	3524	547
11/07/2002	4230	23/01/2007	6228	1998
16/08/2007	5860	05/10/2007	6596	736
19/11/2007	6121	30/09/2014	6623	502
			Total gains	5766

Out of the market

Sell date	Sell price	Buy date	Buy price	Price gain
21/11/1985	1443	28/10/1987	1658	215
11/07/1989	2251	09/04/1990	2228	-23
24/12/1993	3412	07/03/1995	2977	-435
12/10/1995	3524	11/07/2002	4230	706
23/01/2007	6228	16/08/2007	5860	-368
05/10/2007	6596	19/11/2007	6121	-475
			Total gains	-380

Using the FTSE 100 buy and sell signals to buy and sell the FTSE 250

As can be seen from figure 5, the peaks and troughs of the FTSE 250 (top line) correspond fairly closely to those of the FTSE 100 (bottom line). This means, at least in theory, the Market Valuation System's buy and sell triggers for the FTSE 100 could also be used to buy and sell the FTSE 250.

FIGURE 5. PRICE TRENDS OF THE FTSE 100 AND FTSE 250

Table 4 shows the results of using the FTSE 100 market valuation buy/sell signals as triggers to buy and sell the FTSE 250. The results are again striking and clearly show that the FTSE 100 system is effective in determining buy and sell points for the FTSE 250:

- Every single purchase made a capital gain on the subsequent sale.

- Capital losses occurred during four out of the five out-of-market periods.

- Total capital gains during the in-market periods were 14,586.

- The out-of-market periods suffered a total net capital loss of 1166.

These buy/sell signals clearly work and form the basis of the FTSE 250 investment strategies described in Strategies 4 and 6.

TABLE 4. TRACK RECORD OF USING THE FTSE 100 VALUATION SYSTEM BUY AND SELL SIGNALS FOR THE FTSE 250

In the market

Buy date	Buy price	Sell date	Sell price	Price gain
28/10/1987	1959	11/07/1989	2643	684
09/04/1990	2418	24/12/1993	3773	1356
07/03/1995	3330	12/10/1995	3936	607
11/07/2002	5065	23/01/2007	11102	6037
16/08/2007	10463	05/10/2007	11390	928
19/11/2007	10405	30/09/2014	15380	4975
			Total gains	14586

Out of the market

Sell date	Sell price	Buy date	Buy price	Price gain
11/07/1989	2643	09/04/1990	2418	-226
24/12/1993	3773	07/03/1995	3330	-443
12/10/1995	3936	11/07/2002	5065	1129
23/01/2007	11102	16/08/2007	10463	-640
05/10/2007	11390	19/11/2007	10405	-986
			Total gains	-1166

Notes

- FTSE 100 percentage valuations, using the 105%/95% buy/sell spread, provide the buy and sell triggers.

- Although the FTSE 250 index commenced in 1986, the first purchase did not occur until 1987 because the FTSE 100 valuation did not reach 105% until then.

- The price at 30 September 2014 is a hold rather than a sale since a sell signal had not yet occurred following the previous purchase.

Using peak and trough valuations to validate the system

In addition to the track records given in the previous section to validate the Market Valuation System, it is instructive to see the valuations for the FTSE 100 at peak and trough points. If, as some claim, market prices are always based on perfect information and can never, therefore, be regarded as either cheap or expensive, there would be no correlation between the System's valuations and subsequent FTSE 100 performance.

In fact there is a very strong correlation. We have already seen that the System correctly indicated how cheap the FTSE 100 was at the lowest point reached during the credit crunch. I will now show the valuations provided by the System:

- At the highest price ever achieved by the FTSE 100 on 30 December 1999.

- At the subsequent low point reached, after the crash, on 12 March 2003.

Both these valuations use the prevailing annual long-term real dividend growth rate of 2%.

VALUATION FOR THE PEAK CLOSING PRICE OF THE FTSE 100 ON 30 DECEMBER 1999

FIGURE 6. VALUATION OF THE FTSE 100 ON 30 DECEMBER 1999

	A	B	C	D
1				
2	**FTSE 100 VALUATION**			
3				
4	INPUT DATA	Value	RESULTS	Value
5				
6	Date	30-Dec-99	Current Dividend	141.4
7			Inflation Growth Factor	1.038
8			Real Dividend Growth Factor	1.02
9			Actual Dividend Growth Rate % pa	5.83
10	Price	6930.2	End-period Dividend	187.6
11			End-period Dividend Yield %	3.73
12	Dividend Yield %	2.04	End-period FTSE 100 price	5025
13			Average Dividend Yield %	2.89
14	Average Inflation Rate	3.75	End-period Investment Value	5793
15	End-Period Inflation Rate	4.32	Discounted EP Investment Value	4311
16			**Current Intrinsic FTSE 100 Value**	**3919**
17	Real Dividend Growth Rate % pa	2.00	**Current FTSE 100 Value/Price %**	**57**
18				
19	Risk Premium %	10.00	Price to reach 95% Valuation	4125
20			Price to reach 105% Valuation	3732
21	Redemption Yld % pa 5-yr Gilts	6.09		
22			Start Period Investment Value	-6930
23	Notional Investment Start Date	01/01/2000	End Period Investment Value	5793
24	Notional Investment End Date	01/01/2005	**Annual Investment Growth %**	**-3.5**

The Market Valuation System correctly showed that the FTSE 100 price on 30 December 1999 was far too dear. Prices had been driven far too high by dot. com mania. The price subsequently crashed by more than 50% to a low of 3287 on 12 March 2003.

VALUATION FOR THE TROUGH FTSE 100 CLOSING PRICE REACHED ON 12 MARCH 2003

FIGURE 7. VALUATION OF THE FTSE 100 ON 12 MARCH 2003

	A	B	C	D
1				
2	**FTSE 100 VALUATION**			
3				
4	**INPUT DATA**	**Value**	**RESULTS**	**Value**
5				
6	Date	12-Mar-03	Current Dividend	139.4
7			Inflation Growth Factor	1.025
8			Real Dividend Growth Factor	1.02
9			Actual Dividend Growth Rate % pa	4.53
10	Price	3287	End-period Dividend	173.9
11			End-period Dividend Yield %	3.21
12	Dividend Yield %	4.24	End-period FTSE 100 price	5425
13			Average Dividend Yield %	3.72
14	Average Inflation Rate	2.48	End-period Investment Value	6513
15	End-Period Inflation Rate	2.47	Discounted EP Investment Value	5450
16			**Current Intrinsic FTSE 100 Value**	**4954**
17	Real Dividend Growth Rate % pa	2.00	**Current FTSE 100 Value/Price %**	**151**
18				
19	Risk Premium %	10.00	Price to reach 95% Valuation	5215
20			Price to reach 105% Valuation	4718
21	Redemption Yld % pa 5-yr Gilts	3.63		
22			Start Period Investment Value	-3287
23	Notional Investment Start Date	01/01/2000	End Period Investment Value	6513
24	Notional Investment End Date	01/01/2005	**Annual Investment Growth %**	**14.6**

The dot.com bubble burst and prices crashed. As generally happens when bubbles burst, panic set in and prices dropped too far. The FTSE 100 valuation on 12 March 2003 clearly showed this. The valuation of 4954 indicated that prices would have to increase by over 50% to reach fair value. Prices subsequently soared and reached this price in less than two years, on 7 February 2005.

Incidentally, the predicted FTSE 100 price in five years' time, on 12 March 2008, was 5425. The actual price was 5776, less than 7% higher. Most professional analysts cannot predict the FTSE 100 price one year ahead to within 10% of the actual outcome, let alone five years ahead.

2. Comparing five-year investment returns with other investments

The second main use of the valuation system is to compare the five-year annual return of a FTSE 100 investment with returns from alternative investment options, such as a five-year fixed-rate cash deposit. It is important to stress that the risk premium is not taken into account when calculating the annual investment growth figures. It is only used for calculating the current intrinsic value of the FTSE 100. As previously mentioned, you can apply your own personal risk premium to adjust investment growth figures. I will give an example of this later.

To demonstrate how you can use the valuation system for investment decisions, I will use the FTSE 100 valuation of 17 October 2014. First you need to prepare a core valuation for this date, as shown in figure 8.

Core FTSE 100 Valuation

The core valuation of the FTSE 100 on 17 October 2014, using the data prevailing at that date, is shown below. A 0% real annual dividend growth has been assumed in B17, for the reasons discussed previously in this chapter, for the calculation of the Real Dividend Growth Rate.

FIGURE 8. VALUATION OF THE FTSE 100 ON 17 OCTOBER 2014

◇	A	B	C	D
1				
2	**FTSE 100 VALUATION**			
3				
4	INPUT DATA	Value	RESULTS	Value
5				
6	Date	17-Oct-14	Current Dividend	232.2
7			Inflation Growth Factor	1.025
8			Real Dividend Growth Factor	1.00
9			Actual Dividend Growth Rate % pa	2.45
10	Price	6310.3	End-period Dividend	262.1
11			End-period Dividend Yield %	3.33
12	Dividend Yield %	3.68	End-period FTSE 100 price	7861
13			Average Dividend Yield %	3.51
14	Average Inflation Rate	2.45	End-period Investment Value	9339
15	End-Period Inflation Rate	2.92	Discounted EP Investment Value	8673
16			**Current Intrinsic FTSE 100 Value**	**7885**
17	Real Dividend Growth Rate % pa	0.00	**Current FTSE 100 Value/Price %**	**125**
18				
19	Risk Premium %	10.00	Price to reach 95% Valuation	8300
20			Price to reach 105% Valuation	7509
21	Redemption Yld % pa 5-yr Gilts	1.49		
22			Start Period Investment Value	-6310
23	Notional Investment Start Date	01/01/2000	End Period Investment Value	9339
24	Notional Investment End Date	01/01/2005	**Annual Investment Growth %**	**8.1**

The projected annual investment growth is 8.1%. This takes into account basic UK tax on reinvested dividends. It does not take into account any higher rate tax, capital gains tax or personal risk premium. At this date, the best available five-year fixed-rate cash deposit provided an annual return of 3% gross, or 2.4% net of basic rate tax. This return is less than a third of the projected annual return from the FTSE 100 investment. If you are a higher rate taxpayer, you can use the **Personal Projected Post-Tax Annual Investment Growth** section of the spreadsheet to calculate your projected annual investment return after tax. This is shown in figure 9.

FIGURE 9. PERSONALISED INVESTMENT GROWTH PROJECTION OF FTSE 100 VALUATION ON 17 OCTOBER 2014

◇	A	B	C	D
26	**PERSONAL PROJECTED POST-TAX ANNUAL INVESTMENT GROWTH**			
27	Key: PIV = End-period Personal Investment Value, PRP = Personal Risk Premium HR = Higher Rate			
28				
29	Personal extra HR tax on divs	25	PIV post HR tax on dividends	8950
30	Personal Risk Premium	0	PIV post HR tax and PRP	8950
31	Personal CGT %	0	End-period FTSE 100 price post PRP	7861
32			Capital Gain ex reinvested dividends	1550
33			CGT on gain ex dividend reinvestmen	0
34			Net divs received post HR tax	1090
35			% Capital Gains ex reinvested divs	25
36			Estimated Capital Gain on divs	134
37			Estimated CGT on divs	0
38			Total CGT payable	0
39			Start period investment value	-6310
40			PIV ex HR tax, CGT and PRP	8950
41			**Annual Personal Investment Grth**	**7.2**

You can see that inputting the standard extra higher rate tax on dividends of 25% reduces the projected annual investment growth to 7.2%. The annual return from the cash deposit is a mere 1.8% after the deduction of standard UK higher rate tax. This is less than a quarter of the projected annual return from the FTSE 100.

Worst-case scenario valuation

Before making any investment decisions, it is wise to calculate a worst-case scenario for the projected annual return from the investment in the FTSE 100. Leaving aside any personal risk premium which you might wish to apply and your personal tax rates, there are only three input values which you can change from the core valuation:

1. Real dividend growth rate %

2. Average-period inflation %

3. End-period inflation %

The most important of these is the real dividend growth rate. Since the start of the FTSE 100, the worst five-year real dividend growth rate has been -3% annually. It is therefore reasonable to use this as a worst-case scenario.

As regards inflation, valuations will reduce as inflation increases. Inflation has been very low over the last ten years and it is difficult to envisage it increasing beyond 4% annually, especially as the Bank of England is charged with targeting 2%. So, 4% is a reasonable worst-case scenario for the End-period inflation %. The inflation (RPI) rate on 17 October 2014 was 2.3%. It makes sense to assume that average-period inflation will be the average of the start and end figures for the period – namely (2.3+4.0)/2 = 3.15%.

Using these worst-case assumptions in the FTSE 100 valuation reduces the projected annual investment growth for the basic rate taxpayer, excluding any personal risk premium and capital gains tax, to 3.9%, as shown in figure 10. This is still considerably higher than the best available post-tax fixed deposit cash rate of 2.4% annually. Remember, small differences in annual percentages make a big difference to ultimate returns over a number of years. £1,000 would over five years become £1,211 at 3.9% and £1,126 at 2.4%, i.e. the gain would be 67% greater ((211-126)/126 = 0.67).

FIGURE 10. WORST-CASE SCENARIO FTSE 100 VALUATION FOR 17 OCTOBER 2014

◇	A	B	C	D
1				
2	**FTSE 100 VALUATION**	**WORST CASE SCENARIO**		
3				
4	**INPUT DATA**	Value	RESULTS	Value
5	Date	17-Oct-14	Current Dividend	232.2
6				
7			Inflation Growth Factor	1.032
8			Real Dividend Growth Factor	0.97
9			Actual Dividend Growth Rate % pa	0.06
10	Price	6310.3	End-period Dividend	232.9
11			End-period Dividend Yield %	3.64
12	Dividend Yield %	3.68	End-period FTSE 100 price	6392
13			Average Dividend Yield %	3.66
14	Average Inflation Rate	3.15	End-period Investment Value	7651
15	End-Period Inflation Rate	4.00	Discounted EP Investment Value	7106
16			**Current Intrinsic FTSE 100 Value**	**6460**
17	Real Dividend Growth Rate % pa	-3.00	**Current FTSE 100 Value/Price %**	**102**
18				
19	Risk Premium %	10.00	Price to reach 95% Valuation	6800
20			Price to reach 105% Valuation	6152
21	Redemption Yld % pa 5-yr Gilts	1.49		
22			Start Period Investment Value	-6310
23	Notional Investment Start Date	01/01/2000	End Period Investment Value	7651
24	Notional Investment End Date	01/01/2005	**Annual Investment Growth %**	**3.9**

Including a personal risk premium of 10% and the standard rate of UK higher rate tax from reinvested dividends reduces the projected annual investment growth to 1.1%, as shown in figure 11. This is lower than the projected annual cash deposit rate, post higher rate tax, of 1.8%.

However, adding a personal risk premium on top of a worst-case scenario is an extremely pessimistic thing to do. You have to be careful that you do not let excessive risk-aversion steer you away from sensible investment decisions. Without the personal risk premium, the projected annual investment growth for a higher rate taxpayer is 3.0%, considerably higher than that available from fixed rate cash.

FIGURE 11. ADDING A PERSONAL RISK PREMIUM TO THE WORST-CASE FTSE 100 SCENARIO FOR 17 OCTOBER 2014

25				
26	**PERSONAL PROJECTED POST-TAX ANNUAL INVESTMENT GROWTH**			
27	Key: PIV = End-period Personal Investment Value, PRP = Personal Risk Premium HR = Higher Rate			
28				
29	Personal extra HR tax on divs	25	PIV post HR tax on dividends	7320
30	Personal Risk Premium	10	PIV post HR tax and PRP	6654
31	Personal CGT %	0	End-period FTSE 100 price post PRP	5811
32			Capital Gain ex reinvested dividends	-499
33			CGT on gain ex dividend reinvestment	0
34			Net divs received post HR tax	843
35			% Capital Gains ex reinvested divs	-8
36			Estimated Capital Gain on divs	0
37			Estimated CGT on divs	0
38			Total CGT payable	0
39			Start period investment value	-6310
40			PIV ex HR tax, CGT and PRP	6654
41			**Annual Personal Investment Grth**	**1.1**

CHAPTER 3. ADDING MARKET MOMENTUM TO THE VALUATION SYSTEM

There are times when the market gets gripped by panic and prices go into freefall, irrespective of the intrinsic valuations. We have seen examples of this in the previous chapter, when sharp falls have made the market very cheap. In circumstances like this, it makes sense to batten down the hatches and wait until the panic subsides. This chapter describes a technique which can normally cushion you from the worst of these falls and which will almost certainly give you some protection in the event of the market falling more than 50%.

The technique uses market momentum, which measures the trend of the market, either up or down. The momentum is identified by moving averages of price, which smooth the daily price fluctuations. There is a wide range of moving averages that can be applied to price data. In addition, you have the choice of the number of days for which the moving average is calculated. My method employs **simple moving averages**. For example, the 100 day moving average is the simple unweighted average of the closing prices over the last 100 trading days. It is unweighted because each of the 100 prices has an equal weighting in calculating the average.

My method uses moving averages for both 100 and 200 days. These moving averages can be charted, as shown in the example below. The jagged lines are the daily fluctuations in price of the FTSE 100 and the smooth lines are the moving averages. Where the moving averages cross, these points can be used as trigger points in a market momentum system, as follows:

- When the 100 day moving average crosses below the 200 day moving average, this is an indication that the market is trending down.

- When the 100 day moving average crosses above the 200 day moving average, this is an indication that the market is trending upwards.

Note: Readers of *How to Value Shares and Outperform the Market* may have noticed that in that book I used 145 day and 242 day moving averages for this strategy. Here I have changed the moving averages to standard 100 day and 200 day. The principal reason for making this change is to avoid the impression that I cherry-picked 145 day and 242 day averages to achieve favourable historical outcomes.

This market momentum system uses the following steps:

1. Note the market closing price when the 100 day moving average crosses below the 200 day moving average.

2. Calculate 90% of this price.

3. As soon as the market falls to or below this price, and before the 100 day moving average starts moving up again, exit the market. Note that this occurrence happens very rarely and, if you are using the Stock Market Valuation System, you may already be out of the market at this stage.

4. If the 90% market exit trigger has occurred, re-enter the market only when both the 100 day moving average rises above the 200 day moving average and the Stock Market Valuation System is showing a valuation of at least 105%.

You do not have to chart the moving averages yourself by hand, as free services such as Digital Look (www.digitallook.com) and subscriber services such as ShareScope (www.sharescope.co.uk) will provide moving average charts to your own specification.

Using Digital Look to construct moving average charts for the FTSE 100

If you wish to use Digital Look's free service to create a moving average chart for the FTSE 100, follow these simple steps:

1. On the Digital Look website (www.digitallook.com) go to the page for the FTSE 100 index. You can find this by clicking on FTSE 100 in the middle column of the main page, or by entering 'FTSE 100' in the search box that says 'Name or Ticker' towards the top of the page. You can also navigate straight to the page: www.digitallook.com/index/FTSE_100

2. Scroll down until you see a row of buttons that state 'Summary', 'Price', 'Charts', etc. Click on 'Charts'.

3. When the new page opens, scroll down again until you see the heading 'Interactive Chart'. This is the latest price chart for the FTSE 100 and it will

refresh every few minutes. The chart's default setting is to show daily price movements – you can see the word Daily in the top-left corner – which is what we want.

4. Above the chart there is a row of buttons. Click on the one that shows a plus symbol in its top-left corner and a pair of wavy lines. This is the 'Add Indicator' button.

5. A box will pop up with a long list of the many available indicators that can be displayed on the chart. We are interested in simple moving averages for 100 and 200 days, so scroll down the list until you see 'Moving Average – Simple'. You can also type this into the search box above the list.

6. Click on 'Moving Average – Simple' and under the parameters, in the field for Period, enter 100. This will construct a simple moving average for the last 100 days. You may wish to alter the colour of the line to make it clearer. To do this, click on Style and then the coloured box. Select a colour and then press OK. The 100 day moving average will be displayed on the chart.

7. Now repeat step 4 onwards, but instead of entering '100' under Period, enter 200. This will produce a 200 day moving average and overlay this on the chart. If you use a different colour line to that for the 100 day moving average this will make the chart easier to read.

8. You now have a chart of the FTSE 100 price and two moving averages.

Market Momentum System: Example 1

Figure 12 – a chart of the 2007/8 credit crunch crash – shows the Market Momentum System in action (the smooth lines are the moving averages and the jagged line shows the end-of-day closing prices):

• The 100 day moving average crosses below the 200 day moving average on 15 November 2007, when the closing FTSE 100 price is 6359.6.

• 90% of this price is 5723.6.

• The FTSE 100 falls to or below this price on 21 January 2008, when the 100 day moving average is still falling. The closing price is 5578.2. At this point you exit the market.

• The 100 day moving average rises above the 200 day moving average on 28 July 2009, when the closing price is 4528.8. At this price you re-enter the market.

The net effect of this strategy is that you have sold at 5578.2 and re-entered the market at a cheaper price, for 4528.8. This means that you have increased the capital value of your fund by 23.2% compared with sitting on your hands (((5578.2/4528.8) x 100) - 100).

It is also worth pointing out that there was a major one-day fall of 323 points on 21 January 2008, which is why the closing price of 5578.2 is so far below the target exit price of 5723.6. If you had placed a stop-loss of 5724 with your broker in advance, you would probably have achieved a higher exit price than 5578.2, thereby enhancing your return.

FIGURE 12. MARKET MOMENTUM SYSTEM, EXAMPLE 1

To get the net effect of following the strategy, you also have to take into account the value of dividends lost through being out of the market, offset by the value of cash interest earned on an instant-access cash account. Taking into account:

- the time out of the market

- the FTSE 100 dividend yields for this period

- instant-access account interest rates, post the basic rate of tax, for this period (the pre-tax interest rate is assumed to be base rate less 0.5%)

the net loss of income through exiting the market is calculated to be 5.46%. So the net increase to your fund through following the strategy would be 17.74% (23.2% less 5.46%).

Market Momentum System: Example 2

The second example of the Market Momentum System is taken from the 1970s, when the UK stock market crashed by more than 72%. This is considerably greater than any crash which has occurred since the inception of the FTSE 100 in 1984. Although the FTSE 100 index did not exist in the 1970s, there were other UK stock market indices. ShareScope provides a continuous time series of UK stock market prices since 1962. The market peaked at 684.5 on 3 May 1972 and crashed to a low of 188.9 on 18 November 1974, an overall crash of 72.4%.

You can see from figure 13 that this market momentum system would have protected you from the full impact of this cataclysmic crash:

- The 100 day moving average falls below the 200 day moving average on 19 September 1972, when the closing price was 611.

- 90% of this price is 550.

- The price falls to 544.6 on 13 February 1973, when you exit the market.

- The 100 day moving average rises above the 200 day moving average on 10 March 1975, when the price is 373.5. You re-enter the market at this price.

The net effect of this strategy is that you have sold at 544.6 and re-entered the market at 373.5. This means that you would have increased the capital value of your fund by 45.8%, compared with sitting on your hands (((544.6/373.5) x 100) - 100). Dividend yield or interest information for this period is not available, but even if we could make these adjustments they would not be large enough to negate the enormous capital benefit of this strategy.

FIGURE 13. MARKET MOMENTUM SYSTEM, EXAMPLE 2

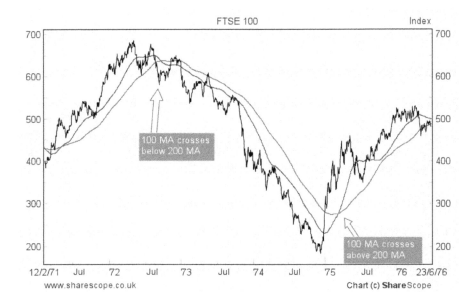

You can follow a similar market momentum strategy for the FTSE 250.

As I have stressed previously, the exit and re-entry signals for this strategy do not happen very often, since this is primarily a strategy to protect you from the impact of major market falls. If you are combining this strategy with the market valuation signals, as described in Strategies 3 and 4, you may already be out of the market, because of the valuation exit signal, when the market momentum exit signal occurs.

Complete record of the Market Momentum System for the FTSE 100 and FTSE 250

The full records of the FTSE 100 and FTSE 250 exit and re-entry signals are shown in Table 5. The final row of each table shows the accumulated compounded increase in value through adopting this strategy since the inception of each index up to 30 September 2014, compared with Strategies 1a and 2a, where you remain fully invested at all times.

TABLE 5. MARKET MOMENTUM SYSTEM EXITS AND RE-ENTRIES FOR THE FTSE 100 AND FTSE 250

FTSE 100: MARKET MOMENTUM SYSTEM EXITS AND RE-ENTRIES

Sell date	Sell price	Buy date	Buy price	% increase in capital	% adj. for dividends and cash	Net % increase in value
14/03/01	5626.0	30/04/02	5165.6	+8.91	+1.0	+ 9.91
15/07/02	3994.5	18/07/03	4073.2	-1.93	-0.89	- 2.82
21/01/08	5578.2	28/07/09	4528.8	+23.17	-5.46	+17.71
					Accumulated increase in value	+25.73

FTSE 250: MARKET MOMENTUM SYSTEM EXITS AND RE-ENTRIES

Sell date	Sell price	Buy date	Buy price	% increase in capital	% adj. for dividends and cash	Net % increase in value
26/04/90	2339.6	08/04/91	2562.9	-8.7	+6.7	- 2.0
22/03/01	5929.8	21/03/02	6125.6	- 3.2	+0.7	- 2.5
24/09/02	4304.8	27/06/03	4958.7	-13.2	-0.5	- 13.7
07/01/08	10093.1	18/06/09	7241.7	+39.4	-1.6	+37.8
					Accumulated increase in value	+13.6

Note: For the column '% adj. for dividends and cash' in Table 5, the adjustment takes into account that, when you sell your holding for a cash deposit, you lose dividend income but gain interest income, compared with staying in the market.

PART B.
SEVEN STRATEGIES

CHAPTER 4. STRATEGY 1 – LONG-TERM INVESTMENT IN THE FTSE 100

This strategy and the next one, Long-term Investment in the FTSE 250, are the simplest strategies to execute and require the least effort. They are only suitable for long-term investment of at least five years since, in the short term, there can be sharp falls in the price of the FTSE 100 and FTSE 250.

This is clear from figure 14, which shows FTSE 100 share price fluctuations. Indeed, had you invested in the FTSE 100 at its all-time closing high of 6930 on 30 December 1999, you would have had to wait seven years for your investment, including net reinvested dividends, to surpass in value your original investment.

So far, nearly 15 years later, the December 1999 all-time closing high of the FTSE price has yet to be surpassed. However, because of the power of reinvested dividends, that original investment of 6930 would now be worth £10,022. That equates to a compound annual return of 2.45%, net of the UK basic rate of income tax. This return over a 15-year period is very much a worst-case scenario for FTSE 100 investment, since, as explained in the previous chapter, the FTSE 100 price on 30 December 1999 was so expensive that investment then would have been foolish.

FIGURE 14. FTSE 100 PRICES SINCE INCEPTION

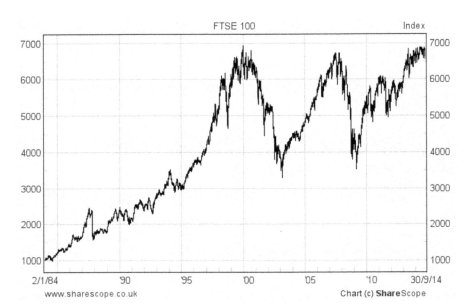

How to maintain a long-term investment in the FTSE 100

It is impractical for a private investor to invest in all 100 companies in the FTSE 100. There are realistically three options for maintaining a long-term investment in the FTSE 100:

1. A FTSE 100 tracker in the form of a unit trust or OEIC (see the glossary in the Appendix).

2. A FTSE 100 exchange traded fund (ETF).

3. Running a synthetic FTSE 100 tracker fund through financial spread trading, as described in Strategy 7.

The benefits and disadvantages of option 3 are described in the chapter on Strategy 7. Here I will cover the relative merits of options 1 and 2. I refer to the current costs of these options, but this is a fast-changing market and you should check the prevailing costs at the time you decide to invest.

Disadvantages of unit trust and OEIC investments

Option 1 is superficially attractive because quoted annual charges from the fund manager can be as low as 0.1%. However, what you should focus on is the year-by-year performance of the fund against the performance of the FTSE 100 index. This includes hidden costs and any error in tracking the index. These performance figures are normally available from the fund's website.

Even for a fund with a low quoted cost, underperformance typically is at least 0.30% per year. On top of this effective fund cost, you will normally have to pay an annual fee to the broker through whom you purchase the fund. Typically these fees range between 0.35% and 0.45% of the value of your fund. So the total cost taken from the value of your fund is likely to be between 0.65% and 0.75%. This means the overall shortfall between the increase in value of the FTSE 100 index and the increase in the value of your FTSE 100 tracker fund could be quite high and increase dramatically over the longer term.

Another major disadvantage of unit trusts or OEICs is that purchases and sales are always conducted on a 'forward price' basis. Prices are normally set around midday but you do not know what that price is going to be when you contract to buy or sell. This means that you can be at the mercy of a falling market and that you cannot effectively implement a damage limitation strategy in a free-falling market, as described in Chapter 3.

Maintaining an investment using an ETF

For all the above reasons, if you decide that Strategy 7 (creating a synthetic FTSE 100 position through financial spread trading) is not for you, I recommend maintaining a FTSE 100 position through a FTSE 100 ETF for Strategies 1 and 3. The ETF structure offers the following advantages:

- You always know the price at which you are buying or selling and the spread between the buying and selling price of a FTSE 100 ETF is normally quite narrow (about 0.03%).

- There is no stamp duty to be paid on purchasing an ETF (for the purchase of individual company shares stamp duty is 0.5%).

- Some of the largest brokers, e.g. Hargreaves Lansdown, charge no annual fee for ETF investments.

- There is no initial charge loaded on to the price of the ETF.

ETF fund managers quote the total expenses which they deduct from the fund value via a percentage total expense ratio (TER). At face value these can be low, as little as 0.1% per year. However, these do not include all the costs of the fund, nor do they take into account how well the fund tracks the FTSE 100. I recommend that instead, you look at the percentage difference in the price of the fund compared with the performance of the index for each of the past few years. I give an example of this below.

Choosing the right FTSE 100 ETF

It is important that you choose the right type of FTSE 100 ETF. The relevant information can be found online from the prospectus of the provider:

- The ETF must invest physically in the constituent shares of the FTSE 100. This reduces your risk. Some FTSE 100 ETFs invest in derivatives. This exposes you to the risk that the derivatives do not match the performance of the FTSE 100. There is a further risk that the provider of the derivatives contracts may default.

- Ensure that the ETF is aiming to match the performance of the FTSE 100 and is not following a leverage strategy, which could result in major underperformance.

- Most ETFs have offshore status. Ensure that your ETF has *reporting status*. This means that any capital gains will be taxed at capital gains tax rates, rather than the currently higher income tax rates.

A FTSE 100 ETF which ticks all these boxes, and has a low-cost structure, is the i-Shares FTSE 100 UCITS ETF – code ISF. It is provided by BlackRock, one of the biggest fund managers in the world. Opt for automated dividend reinvestment via your online broker. The brokers I recommend in Part C charge around 1% of the value of each dividend reinvested.

From its prospectus, the performance of this ETF, compared with the total return of the FTSE 100 (including reinvested dividends) for each of the past four years to 30 September is shown in table 6.

So the average annual underperformance of this ETF over the last four years has been 0.46%. This takes into account all of the costs of the ETF and any tracking error in tracking the performance of the FTSE 100. This is a low price to pay compared with the total costs including broker fees of FTSE 100 trackers provided by unit trusts or OEICs.

TABLE 6. TOTAL RETURNS OF THE I-SHARES FTSE 100 UCITS ETF V FTSE 100

Year to 30 September	2011	2012	2013	2014	Average
FTSE 100 Total Return %	-4.41	+16.36	+16.74	+6.13	
i-Shares FTSE 100 UCITS performance %	-4.89	+15.87	+16.29	+5.71	
i-Shares underperformance %	0.48	0.49	0.45	0.42	0.46

Long-term historic returns of cost-effective investment in the FTSE 100

Although the i-Shares FTSE 100 ETF has only become available in recent years, it is possible to replicate the long-term return of investment in the FTSE 100 since 1984, by applying the same cost structure, including the cost of reinvested dividends, as described in the previous section.

The FTSE 100 capital value at the start of 1984 was 1000 (by definition). By 30 September 2014, this capital value had increased to 6622.7. The value of reinvested dividends, less the above annual fund costs of 0.46% and transaction costs for dividend reinvestment, would have increased this latter capital value by 128.2%, increasing the capital value to 15,113. This equates to a compound annual actual return of **9.23%**.

This return includes reinvested dividends taxed at the basic rate of UK income tax.

Compound annual inflation (RPI) over this period was 3.58%, making the compound annual real long-term return **5.45%**.[4]

This return is considerably higher than the real long-term return which a cash deposit would have delivered. The long-term real annual return of a UK cash deposit has varied between 1.3% (20 years) and 1.5% (50 years), according to the Barclays Capital Equity Gilt study. Even using the higher figure of 1.5% provides an actual annual cash return of 5.13%, after adding back inflation. This is a pre-tax return and so, to compare with the after-tax FTSE 100 return, it needs to be adjusted for the current UK basic rate of income tax (20%), making 4.1%.

---

4 The 5.45% is obtained by discounting the 9.23% by 3.58%, as in $(1.0923/1.0358) = 1.0545$. All adjustments from actual to real percentages take inflation into account in this way rather than subtracting the inflation percentage from the actual percentage.

The real cash return of 1.5% reduces to 1.2%, after the deduction of basic rate UK tax. This compares with the equivalent real post-tax return of 5.45% from this strategy.

On an initial deposit of £1000 at the start of 1984, this compound actual annual return from cash would have delivered only £3,440 by 30 September 2014. *This amount is less than 23% of the £15,113 delivered by the FTSE 100 accumulated fund.*

A small difference in the compound annual return will make a big difference to the long-term accumulated fund.

The above comparison of the respective accumulated funds produced by long-term FTSE 100 investment and long-term cash deposit investment underlines a very important principle which runs throughout this book: small differences in annual returns make big differences in long-term fund values.

For example, a compound annual return of 10% is double the compound annual return of 5.0%. However, after 30 years of compounding, the higher return will produce an accumulated fund more than quadruple the size of the lower return.

Prospective future returns from this strategy

The future returns from this strategy will depend on two factors:

1. The rate of capital (price) growth of the FTSE 100.
2. The dividend yield of the FTSE 100.

The capital growth of the FTSE 100 is closely tied to the dividend growth of the FTSE 100, as I explained in the chapter on the Stock Market Valuation System. Since 1984, the real compound annual growth of the FTSE 100 has averaged 2.5%, but has been on a steadily declining trend. I think it is therefore reasonable to assume that in the future there will be 0% real growth in the FTSE 100 dividend and, consequently, in the FTSE 100 price. This means that, although there will be the usual swings in price driven by fear and greed, the long-term trend will be for the price increase to match inflation.

As regards the FTSE 100 dividend yield, the net dividend yield after basic rate tax has averaged 3.17% since 1984. This is 0.41% below the average inflation rate for the period of 3.58%, i.e. a negative real dividend yield. However, in the last few years the real dividend yield has turned positive. The reason for this increase in the real dividend yield is the reduction in the real dividend growth rate, which I discussed in Chapter 2.

In the same way that an annuity which does not offer inflation protection is cheaper to buy than one which does, so the FTSE 100 price will be depressed by a reduction in expected dividend growth. A depression in the FTSE 100 price increases the dividend yield. At the end of September 2014, when market expectations of inflation over the next five years were an average annual rate of 2.7%, the FTSE 100 dividend yield was 3.49%, an implied real return of 0.79%. Erring on the conservative side, I would assume a real FTSE 100 dividend yield in the future of around 0.5%, making an actual dividend yield of 3.2% if inflation is 2.7%.

What does this mean in practice for the prospective long-term returns from FTSE 100 investment using this strategy?

Initial investment	a. 100
FTSE 100 price growth: inflation at 2.7% and 0% real div growth = 2.7%*	b. 102.7
FTSE dividend uplift: 2.71% (3.2% yield net of ETF and reinvestment costs)**	c. 105.5 (b x 1.0271)

* see above

** 3.2% dividend yield less 0.46% ETF costs = 2.74%. Less 1% dividend reinvestment cost = 2.74 x 0.99 = 2.71%

So the prospective actual annual investment return, net of basic rate tax is **5.5%**.

This equates to a prospective real annual return of **2.7%**.

These figures are obviously lower than the historical returns but they are still likely to be much higher than the returns achievable from cash deposits. At the end of September 2014, the best available fixed-rate five year cash deposit was 3.0% annually gross. After the basic rate of tax this equates to 2.4%, less than half the prospective actual return from the FTSE 100 (5.5%), and not even keeping pace with inflation at 2.7%.

Get a FTSE 100 valuation before you invest

I strongly advise you to get a FTSE 100 valuation before you invest, especially if you are considering investing a lump sum for long-term growth. The return which you achieve will be heavily influenced by the value of the FTSE 100 at the time you invest. We saw earlier in this chapter that, if you invested on 30 December 1999 when the FTSE 100 was extremely expensive, it would have taken you seven years to recoup your initial investment and, even over 14 years later, the compound annual return would have been small.

You can easily avoid this mistake by getting a FTSE 100 valuation before you invest. You can get a valuation by building the FTSE 100 valuation spreadsheet, as described in the section on the Stock Market Valuation System. If you do not wish to do this, you can get a current FTSE 100 valuation from ShareMaestro (www.sharemaestro.co.uk). Do not invest unless the FTSE 100 valuation is at least 105%.

Summary of the strategy

1. Place your investment capital in a competitive instant-access cash account.

2. Make a FTSE 100 valuation using the Stock Market Valuation System.

3. If the FTSE 100 valuation in step 2 is lower than 105%, leave your investment capital in the cash account and make periodic valuations until the valuation reaches at least 105%. At that point, follow the steps below.

4. If the valuation in step 2 is at least 105%, invest all your investment capital in a FTSE 100 ETF, as described earlier in this chapter, or invest it in a synthetic FTSE 100 tracker, as described in Strategy 7. If you opt for a FTSE 100 ETF, invest if possible via a tax-free vehicle such as an ISA or a SIPP.

5. If you opt for an ETF as your investment vehicle, ensure that you get dividends automatically reinvested by your broker.

6. Hold your investment for a minimum of five years. You are free to sell all or part of your investment at any time but, the longer you hold, the lower the risk and the higher the potential return.

Strategy 1b. Boosting your returns and reducing your risk

The long-term FTSE 100 investment strategy is designed for minimum effort. You make lump sum investment(s), have dividends automatically reinvested and withdraw some or all of the funds when you need them.

However, with little extra effort, you can boost your returns and lower your risk by following the strategy described in Adding Market Momentum to the Valuation System, in Chapter 3.

The reduction of risk is important for two reasons:

1. It helps reduce your exposure to a major market crash just before you wish to withdraw some or all of your funds.

2. It helps protect your funds from exposure to a cataclysmic crash, such as the Wall Street crash in 1929. As recently as the 1970s, the UK stock market fell by more than 70%. Effective use of the Market Momentum System would have shielded your funds from a large proportion of this crash.

Using the same sell and buy dates as shown in the Market Momentum chapter, the boost to your returns from following this strategy historically is calculated as follows:

TABLE 7. BOOSTING THE RETURNS FROM STRATEGY 1 BY USING THE MARKET MOMENTUM SYSTEM

Sell date	Sell price	Buy date	Buy price	% increase in capital	% adj for divs and cash	Net % increase in value
14/03/01	5626.0	30/04/02	5165.6	+8.91	+1.0	+ 9.91
15/07/02	3994.5	18/07/03	4073.2	-1.93	-0.89	- 2.82
21/01/08	5578.2	28/07/09	4528.8	+23.17	-5.46	+17.71
					Accumulated increase in value	+25.73

The explanation of the last three columns in this table is as follows:

- **% increase in capital**: This is the increase in capital arising from selling shares at one price and buying them back at a lower price. A negative increase occurs when the buy-back price is higher than the selling price.

- **% adjustment for dividends and cash**: This takes into account the dividends lost through exiting the market, offset by investing the cash at an assumed post-tax rate of Base Rate less 0.5%. This rate is lower than long-term fixed rate cash since, to fulfil this strategy, the cash has to be available on an instant-access basis so that it can be reinvested in the FTSE 100 as soon as the market momentum signal indicates that the time is right.

- **Net % increase in value:** This is the net increase in value taking into account the above two factors.

The accumulated increase in value from adopting the market momentum strategy adds 25.73% to the accumulated fund of £15,113,[5] which therefore

---

5 The accumulated fund of £15,113 was achieved on an initial £1000 investment by following a passive FTSE 100 investment strategy from the start of 1984 to the end of September 2014, as described earlier in this chapter.

increases to £19,001. This increased fund equates to a compound annual actual return of **10.0%**.

This is equivalent to a real compound annual return of **6.2%** (net of historic inflation at 3.58%).

Compared with the core Strategy 1, there are the following modifications for operating Strategy 1b:

1. You sell and buy your FTSE 100 investment according to the exit and re-entry signals of the Market Momentum System.

2. As you may be incurring capital gains when you sell, it is especially important, if possible, to hold your FTSE 100 investment via a tax-free vehicle such as an ISA, SIPP or a synthetic FTSE 100 tracker, as described in Strategy 7. When you sell because of a Market Momentum signal, do not withdraw your investment from an ISA or a SIPP as this will destroy the tax-free status of the funds.

CHAPTER 5. STRATEGY 2 – LONG-TERM INVESTMENT IN THE FTSE 250

The FTSE 250 comprises the 250 next most valuable UK companies after the FTSE 100. Like the FTSE 100, it is a weighted index so the larger companies carry more weighting in the pricing of the index.

By definition the FTSE 250 index has smaller companies than the FTSE 100, so its constituent companies have greater scope for growth, and indeed historically the FTSE 250 has outperformed the FTSE 100 by a large margin. Since its inception at the start of 1986 to the end of September 2014, the capital growth of the FTSE 250 has been 967%. Over the same period the capital growth of the FTSE 100 has been 366%.

As a result of this, the historic compound annual real dividend growth rate of the FTSE 250, from the beginning of 1986 when the index started to the end of September 2014, has been 4.62%. This is much higher than that of the FTSE 100.

The capital growth of the FTSE 250 has also been correspondingly higher, as was seen in figure 5 in Chapter 2. Whilst the FTSE 100 has never regained the peak achieved on 30 December 1999, the FTSE 250 peaked on 18 September 2000 at 6901 and surpassed that peak on 30 December 2004. By 30 September 2014 the index had risen strongly to 15,379.

So, while the FTSE 100 gets all the attention, it is the FTSE 250 which is the neglected gem. The higher growth of the FTSE 250 does carry some extra downside risk but, as can be seen in table 8, this is not significant. This table shows the major falls of the FTSE 100 and FTSE 250 in pairs, when at least one of the pair has fallen by 20% or more. It is clear that the additional downside risk of the FTSE 250 in the event of major falls is not excessive.

TABLE 8. LOOKING AT THE MAJOR FALLS OF THE FTSE 250 AND FTSE 100 TO ASSESS THEIR COMPARATIVE DOWNSIDE RISKS

	High date	Price	Low date	Price	% fall
FTSE 100	16/07/1987	2443	04/12/1987	1582	35.2
FTSE 250	09/10/1987	2835	10/11/1987	1700	40.0
FTSE 100	02/02/1994	3520	24/06/1994	2877	18.3
FTSE 250	03/02/1994	4153	09/03/1995	3311	20.3
FTSE 100	30/12/1999	6930	12/03/2003	3287	52.6
FTSE 250	18/09/2000	6901	12/03/2003	3802	44.9
FTSE 100	15/06/2007	6732	03/03/2009	3512	47.8
FTSE 250	23/05/2007	12220	09/03/2009	5770	52.8

How to maintain a long-term investment in the FTSE 250

As with Strategy 1 for the FTSE 100, this strategy invests in the FTSE 250 and stays invested.

For the reasons given in Chapter 4, I recommend using an ETF as the long-term investment vehicle, rather than a unit trust or OEIC. There is also a variation of this strategy using market momentum to cushion the falls of major crashes. As with Strategy 1, this strategy requires little effort.

Choosing the right FTSE 250 ETF

The same factors which guide the choice of a FTSE 100 ETF also guide the choice of a FTSE 250 ETF:

• Tracking accuracy.

• Investment in physical shares rather than derivatives.

- *Reporting status* so that capital gains are taxed as capital gains rather than income.

- Low costs.

The FTSE 250 ETF which most closely matches these criteria is the i-Shares FTSE 250 UCITS ETF (code MIDD). You can instruct your broker to invest dividends automatically for you for a commission of around 1% of the dividend. This cost has been taken into account in constructing the track record of this strategy.

To calculate the effective cost incurred by the fund, compared with the FTSE 250 performance, the best guide, as with the FTSE 100, is to study the tracking record figures produced by i-Shares for this fund.

TABLE 9. TOTAL RETURNS OF THE I-SHARES FTSE 250 UCITS ETF V FTSE 250

Year to 30 September	2011	2012	2013	2014	Average
FTSE 250 Total Return %	-4.19	+23.10	+30.50	+5.86	
i-Shares FTSE 250 performance %	-4.41	+22.50	+29.92	+5.40	
i-Shares underperformance %	0.22	0.60	0.58	0.46	0.465

So the average annual underperformance of this ETF has been 0.465%. This takes into account all the costs of the ETF and any error in tracking the performance of the FTSE 250. This is a low price to pay compared with the total costs, including broker fees, of a FTSE 250 tracker provided by unit trusts or OEICs.

Long-term historic returns of cost-effective investment in the FTSE 250

Although the i-Shares FTSE 250 ETF has only become available in recent years, it is possible to replicate the long-term return of investment in the FTSE 250 since inception in 1986, by applying the same cost structure as described in the previous section.

The FTSE 250 capital value at the start of 1986 was 1440.4. By 30 September 2014, this capital value had increased to 15379.7. The value of reinvested dividends, net of fund and dividend reinvestment costs, would have increased this latter capital value by 97.4%, increasing the capital value to 30359. This equates to a compound annual actual return of **11.18%**.

This return includes reinvested dividends taxed at the basic rate of UK income tax.

Compound annual inflation (RPI) over this period was 3.47%, making the compound annual real long-term return **7.45%**.

This real return is considerably higher than the real long-term return which long-term investment in the FTSE 100 has delivered (5.45% annually). If the FTSE 250 had existed at the start of 1984, when the FTSE 100 commenced, £1,000 invested at this actual annual return of 11.18% would have grown to £26,048 by 30 September 2014. This is 72% higher than the fund accumulated through long-term FTSE 100 investment (£15,113) and over seven times the size of a fund accumulated through long-term cash deposits.

Prospective future returns from this strategy

The future returns from this strategy will depend on two factors:

1. The rate of capital (price) growth of the FTSE 250.

2. The dividend yield of the FTSE 250.

The capital growth of the FTSE 250 is closely tied to the dividend growth of the FTSE 250, as I explained in Chapter 2 on the UK Stock Market Valuation System. Since 1986, the real compound annual growth of the FTSE 250 has averaged 4.6%, but recently has been lower. I think it is reasonable to assume that in the future there will be 2% real growth in the FTSE 250 dividend and, consequently, in the FTSE 250 price. This means, although there will be the usual swings in price driven by fear and greed, the long-term trend will be for the price to beat inflation by 2% per year.

As regards the dividend yield, the net dividend yield has averaged 2.9% since 1986. This is 0.6% below the average inflation rate for the period of 3.5%. However, in the last few years the negative real dividend yield has reduced. The reason for this effective increase in the real dividend yield is the recent reduction in real dividend growth rates, which I discussed in Chapters 2 and 4.

In the same way that an annuity which does not offer inflation protection is cheaper to buy than one which does, so the FTSE 250 price will be depressed by a reduction in expected dividend growth. A depression in the FTSE 250 price increases the dividend yield. At the end of September 2014, when market expectations of inflation over the next five years were an average annual rate of 2.7%, the FTSE 250 dividend yield was 2.6%, giving an implied real return of -0.1%. Erring on the conservative side, I would assume a real FTSE 250 dividend yield in the future of around -0.3%.

What does this mean in practice for the prospective long-term returns from FTSE 250 investment using this strategy?

Initial investment	a. 100
FTSE 250 price growth: inflation at 2.7% and 2% real div growth = 4.7%*	b. 104.7
FTSE 250 dividend uplift: 1.9% (2.4% yield less ETF and reinvestment costs)**	c. 106.7 (b x 1.019)

* see above

** 2.4% dividend yield less 0.465% ETF costs = 1.94%. Less 1% reinvestment cost = 1.9%.

So the prospective actual annual return is **6.7%, net of the basic rate of tax**.

This equates to a prospective real annual return net of inflation at 2.7% of **3.9%**.

These figures are obviously lower than the historical returns but they are still likely to be much higher than the returns achievable from cash deposits. At the end of September 2014, the best available fixed rate five year cash deposit was 3.0% annually gross. After the basic rate of tax this equates to 2.4%, 64% less than the annual prospective actual return from the FTSE 250 and not even keeping pace with the prospective inflation of 2.7%.

Get a FTSE 100 valuation before you invest

The FTSE 250 peaks and troughs closely match those of the FTSE 100 and so you can use the FTSE 100 valuation as a proxy for the FTSE 250 valuation.

I strongly advise you to get a FTSE 100 valuation before you invest, especially if you are considering investing a lump sum for long-term growth. The return which you achieve will be heavily influenced by the percentage valuation of the FTSE 100 at the time you invest. We saw earlier in this chapter that if you invested on 30 December 1999, when the FTSE 100 was extremely expensive, it would have taken you seven years to recoup your initial investment and, even over 14 years later, the compound annual return would have been very small.

You can easily avoid the mistake of investing in the FTSE 250 when the price is too dear by getting a FTSE 100 valuation before you invest. You can get a valuation by building a FTSE 100 valuation spreadsheet, as described in Chapter 2 on the UK Stock Market Valuation System. If you do not wish to do this, you can get a current FTSE 100 valuation from ShareMaestro (www.sharemaestro. co.uk). Do not invest if the FTSE 100 valuation is below 105%.

Summary of the strategy

1. Place your investment capital in a competitive instant-access cash account.

2. Make a FTSE 100 valuation using the Stock Market Valuation System.

3. If the FTSE 100 valuation in step 2 is lower than 105%, leave your investment capital in the cash account and make periodic valuations until the valuation reaches at least 105%. At that point, follow the steps below.

4. If the valuation in step 2 is at least 105%, invest all your investment capital in a FTSE 250 ETF, as described earlier in this chapter. Invest if possible via a tax-free vehicle such as an ISA or a SIPP.

5. Ensure that you get dividends automatically reinvested by your broker.

6. Hold your investment for a minimum of five years. You are free to sell all or part of your investment at any time but, the longer you hold, the lower the risk and the higher the potential return.

Strategy 2b. Boosting your returns and reducing your risk

This long-term FTSE 250 investment strategy is designed for minimum effort. You may make lump sum investment(s), reinvest dividends and withdraw some or all of the funds when you need them. However, with little extra effort, you can boost your returns and lower your risk by following the strategy described in Chapter 3, Adding Market Momentum to the Valuation System.

The reduction of risk is important for two reasons:

1. It helps reduce your exposure to a major market crash just before you wish to withdraw some or all of your funds.

2. It helps protect your funds from exposure to a cataclysmic crash, such as the Wall Street crash in 1929. As recently as the 1970s, the UK stock market fell by more than 70%. Effective use of the Market Momentum System would have shielded your funds from a large proportion of this crash.

The FTSE 250 market momentum strategy has produced four sales and repurchases since 1986. Three of these occasions have produced small negative results but the strategy did succeed in avoiding the major losses of the credit crunch crash. Using the same sell and buy dates for the FTSE 250 as shown in the Market Momentum chapter, the boost to your returns from following this strategy historically is calculated as shown in table 10.

TABLE 10. BOOSTING THE RETURNS FROM STRATEGY 2 BY USING THE MARKET MOMENTUM SYSTEM

Sell date	Sell price	Buy date	Buy price	% increase in capital	% adjustment for dividends and cash	Net % increase in value
26/04/90	2339.6	08/04/91	2562.9	-8.7	+6.7	- 2.0
22/03/01	5929.8	21/03/02	6125.6	- 3.2	+0.7	- 2.5
24/09/02	4304.8	27/06/03	4958.7	-13.2	-0.5	- 13.7
07/01/08	10093.1	18/06/09	7241.7	+39.4	-1.6	+37.8
					Accumulated increase in value	+13.6

The explanation of the last three columns in this table is as follows:

- **% increase in capital:** This is the increase in capital arising from selling shares at one price and buying them back at a lower price. A negative increase occurs when the buy-back price is higher than the selling price.

- **% adjustment for dividends and cash:** This takes into account the dividends lost through exiting the market offset by investing the cash at an assumed post-tax rate of Base Rate less 0.5%. This rate is lower than long-term fixed rate cash since, to fulfil this strategy, the cash has to be available on an instant-access basis so that it can be reinvested in the FTSE 250 as soon as the Market Momentum System indicates that the time is right.

- **Net % increase in value:** This is the net increase in value taking into account the above two factors.

The accumulated increase in value from adopting the market momentum strategy adds 13.6% to the accumulated fund of £30,359, which therefore increases to £34,488. This increased fund equates to a compound annual return, on an initial value of £1,440.4 at the start of 1986, of **11.67%**.

This is a real compound annual return net of historic inflation at 3.47% of **7.92%**.

This is a very strong return which would have considerably surpassed the long-term returns of most UK funds.

Compared with the core Strategy 2, there are the following modifications for operating Strategy 2b:

- You sell and buy your FTSE 250 investment according to the exit and re-entry signals of the Market Momentum System.

- As you may be incurring capital gains when you sell, it is especially important, if possible, to hold your FTSE 250 investment via a tax-free vehicle such as an ISA or SIPP.

- When you sell because of a Market Momentum signal, do not withdraw your investment from an ISA or a SIPP as this will destroy the tax-free status of the funds.

CHAPTER 6. STRATEGY 3 – BOOSTING LONG-TERM INVESTMENT IN THE FTSE 100 WITH MARKET TIMING

Chapter 2 on the UK Stock Market Valuation System described a strategy for buying the FTSE 100 when the intrinsic valuation is at least 105% of the market price and selling when the valuation falls to 95% of the market price. Since the start of the FTSE 100 in 1984, each buy/sell signal has always delivered a capital profit – in other words the price when selling the FTSE 100 has always been higher than when buying. These percentage buy and sell triggers form the backbone of the strategy described in this chapter.

When this strategy is used to invest in the FTSE 100, in addition to any capital gain on sale, it also benefits from the accumulated value of reinvested dividends. When the strategy signals exiting the market, the cash is assumed to be invested in a competitive instant-access cash account, so that the cash is available for reinvestment as soon as the FTSE 100 price becomes good value again (i.e. valuation of 105% or more) and meanwhile earns interest.

For added safety and returns, this strategy also uses the Market Momentum System described in Chapter 3. You may recall that this strategy involves exiting the market when the FTSE 100 price has fallen at least 10% below the point at which the 100 day moving average of FTSE 100 prices crosses below the 200 day moving average. Re-entry to the market occurs when the 100 day moving average crosses above the 200 day moving average.

Overlap between the Market Momentum System and the Stock Market Valuation System

The key reason for combining the Market Momentum System with the Stock Market Valuation System is to protect the value of your fund against large falls in the market which may occur, irrespective of market valuations, when panic sets in.

The overlap of the two systems produces the following rules:

- You exit the market when the FTSE 100 valuation has fallen to 95% or below, even if the Market Momentum System has produced no exit signal.

- You also exit the market when the Market Momentum System produces an exit signal, even if the FTSE 100 valuation has not fallen to 95% or below.

- If you have exited the market because of a signal from the Market Momentum System, you only re-enter the market after the 100 day moving average has crossed upwards above the 200 day moving average **and** when the FTSE 100 valuation is at least 105%.

- If you have exited the FTSE 100 because the valuation has fallen to 95% or below and there subsequently occurs a Market Momentum exit signal, you only re-enter the market when both conditions described in the previous bullet point are met.

Summary of the strategy

This investment strategy can be summarised as follows:

1. Invest in a cost-effective FTSE 100 ETF when the FTSE 100 valuation is at least 105% and the Market Momentum System indicates the market is **not** in freefall.

2. Sell the FTSE 100 ETF when the FTSE 100 price has fallen to 95% or below or when the Market Momentum System indicates the market is in freefall.

3. Invest the sale proceeds in a competitive instant-access cash account until the situation in step 1 prevails again.

4. When a market momentum exit has occurred, only reinvest in the FTSE 100 ETF when both the FTSE 100 valuation is at least 105% and the Market Momentum re-entry signal has occurred.

Track record of the strategy

The track record of this strategy is shown in table 11. The first pair of market momentum exit/re-entry signals was not used. That is because, although there was a market momentum exit signal on 14 March 2001, the FTSE 100 valuation system had already produced an exit signal. Similarly, although there was a market momentum re-entry signal on 30 April 2002, the FTSE 100 valuation system had not yet reached 105% and so re-entry waited until this valuation was reached on 11 July 2002.

Where sell and buy prices are shown in shaded cells in table 11, these indicate respectively occasions when the market momentum system triggered exits and re-entries to the market. So, for example, there was a market momentum exit on 21 January 2008, even though the FTSE 100 value was still above 95%. Re-entry to the market then had to wait until the market momentum re-entry signal occurred on 28 July 2009, even though the FTSE 100 value was above 105% well before this.

As you will see from the track record, there were two occasions when the market momentum system came into play. The first occasion produced a small capital loss as the re-entry price of 4073.2 was slightly higher than the exit price of 3994.5. The second occasion, during the credit crunch, produced a significant capital gain because the re-entry price of 4528.8 was significantly lower than the exit price of 5578.2.

In constructing this track record, I have replicated as closely as possible the actual costs and benefits which would be incurred by the accumulating fund. FTSE 100 investment is assumed to be undertaken via the i-Shares FTSE 100 UCITS ETF, which was recommended in Strategy 1. Dividends are reinvested. Although this ETF was not available in 1984, I have replicated its cost structure across the whole period of FTSE 100 investment in this strategy since 1984. The strategy was in cash initially until the valuation exceeded 105%.

The overall compound actual annual return for this strategy from the start of 1984 to 30 September 2014 has been 10.3%. This is a very strong result, outperforming the vast majority of commercial UK equity funds. Since annual inflation over this period averaged 3.58%, the annual real return has been 6.5%.[6]

The development of the track record follows this pattern:

---

6   The 6.5% is obtained by discounting the 10.3% by 3.58% as in $(1.103/1.0358)=1.065$. All adjustments from actual to real percentages take inflation into account in this way rather than subtracting the inflation percentage from the actual percentage.

- The accumulated value of the initial investment, in the final column, shows the value of the fund when cash has been invested in the FTSE 100 ETF or when the ETF has been sold.

- Interest earned on cash is shown in the penultimate column.

- When the ETF position is sold, this creates a capital gain (or loss) from the difference between the selling price and the buying price. The typical buy/sell price spread for this ETF has also been taken into account.

- To this capital profit has been added the extra value created by reinvested dividends, net of the effective costs charged by the ETF.

- The net capital profit plus the value of reinvested dividends creates a total ETF value which is invested in cash when the ETF position is sold.

- Detailed assumptions are given after the table.

TABLE 11. LONG-TERM TRACK RECORD OF STRATEGY 3

Buy date (price)	Sell date (price)	% capital gain less spread	Capital gain less trans costs	Fund value before reinvested divs	Value of reinvested divs net of fund costs	Net interest	Acc. fund (£)
01/01/84 (fund start)							10,000
						1110	11,110
26/06/85 (1236.5)	21/11/85 (1443.1)	16.7	1827	12937	123		13,060
						1842	14,902
28/10/87 (1658.4)	11/07/89 (2250.9)	35.7	5293	20195	1012		21,207
						1419	22,625
09/04/90 (2227.7)	24/12/93 (3412.3)	53.1	11996	34621	4013		38,634
						1760	40,393
07/03/95 (2977)	12/10/95 (3523.8)	18.3	7380	47773	826		48,600
						15980	64,579
11/07/02 (4230)	15/07/02 (3994.5)	-5.6	-3639	60941	18		60,959

Buy date (price)	Sell date (price)	% capital gain less spread	Capital gain less trans costs	Fund value before reinvested divs	Value of reinvested divs net of fund costs	Net interest	Acc. fund (£)
						1542	62,501
18/07/03 (4073.2)	23/01/07 (6227.6)	52.8	33005	95506	9780		105,286
						2327	107,612
16/08/07 (5859.9)	05/10/07 (6595.8)	12.5	13453	121065	448		121,513
						626	122,139
19/11/07 (6120.8)	21/01/08 (5578.2)	-8.9	-10886	111253	567		111,821
						3625	115,446
28/07/09 (4528.8)	30/09/14 (6622.7)	46.2	53301	168747	35319		204,065
		Compound annual return 1/1/84 to 30/9/14					10.3%

Assumptions

- FTSE 100 closing prices are used for each buy/sell date.

- The price shown for 30/09/2014 is the hold price for the end of the period. It is not a sale price since no sell signal occurred on this date.

- The buy/sell spread is assumed to be 0.03%, based on the current typical spread.

- Each buy/sell transaction costs £12.50.

- Effective fund costs, including tracking errors, are assumed to be 0.46% p.a.

- The percentage increase through reinvested dividends takes into account the prevailing dividend yields, the period of investment and a 1% transaction cost for dividend reinvestment.

- The net interest is based on the UK base rate less 0.5%, taxed at the UK basic rate of tax, and takes into account the period invested.

- The investor is a basic rate UK taxpayer with no capital gains tax liabilities in excess of the CGT threshold.

Future performance prospects

Historically this strategy has produced an annual return about 1% higher than the passive long-term FTSE 100 investment strategy described in Strategy 1 (excluding the market momentum add-on). I would therefore expect future returns to be about 1% higher annually than Strategy 1, meaning a **6.5%** actual return or **3.7%** real return, assuming inflation of 2.7% annually.

CHAPTER 7. STRATEGY 4 – BOOSTING LONG-TERM INVESTMENT IN THE FTSE 250 WITH MARKET TIMING

Chapter 2 described a strategy for buying the FTSE 250 when the FTSE 100 intrinsic valuation is at least 105% of the market price and selling when the valuation falls to 95% of the market price or below.

Since the start of the FTSE 100 in 1984, each buy/sell signal has always delivered a capital profit – in other words the price of the FTSE 250 when selling has always been higher than when buying. These buy and sell triggers form the backbone of the strategy described in this chapter.

When this strategy is used to invest in the FTSE 250, in addition to any capital gain on sale, it also benefits from the accumulated value of reinvested dividends. When the strategy signals exiting the market, the cash is assumed to be invested in a competitive instant-access cash account, so that the cash is available for reinvestment as soon as the FTSE 100 price becomes good value again (i.e. 105% or more) and meanwhile earns interest.

For added safety and returns, this strategy also uses the Market Momentum System described in Chapter 3. You may recall that this strategy involves exiting the market when the FTSE 250 price has fallen at least 10% below the point at which the 100 day moving average of FTSE 250 prices crosses below the 200 day moving average. Re-entry to the market occurs when the 100 day moving average crosses upward above the 200 day moving average.

Overlap between the Market Momentum System and the Stock Market Valuation System

The key reason for combining the Market Momentum System with the Stock Market Valuation System is to protect the value of your fund against large falls in the market which may occur, irrespective of market valuations, when panic sets in.

The overlap of the two systems produces the following rules:

- You exit the market when the FTSE 100 valuation has fallen to 95% or below, even if the FTSE 250 Market Momentum System has produced no exit signal.

- You also exit the market when the FTSE 250 Market Momentum System produces an exit signal, even if the FTSE 100 valuation has not fallen to 95% or below.

- If you have exited the market because of a signal from the FTSE 250 Market Momentum System, you only re-enter the market after the FTSE 250 100 day moving average crosses upward above the 200 day moving average **and** the FTSE 100 valuation is at least 105%.

- When a market momentum exit has occurred, only reinvest in the FTSE 250 ETF when both the FTSE 100 valuation is at least 105% and the Market Momentum re-entry signal has occurred.

Summary of the strategy

This investment strategy can be summarised as follows:

1. Invest in a cost-effective FTSE 250 ETF when the FTSE 100 valuation is at least 105% and the Market Momentum System indicates the market is **not** in freefall.

2. Sell the FTSE 250 ETF when the FTSE 100 price has fallen to 95% or below or when the Market Momentum System indicates the market is in freefall.

3. Invest sale proceeds in a competitive instant-access cash account until the situation in step 1 prevails again.

4. When a market momentum exit has occurred, only reinvest in the FTSE 250 ETF when both the FTSE 100 valuation is at least 105% and the market momentum re-entry signal has occurred.

Track record of the strategy

The track record of this strategy is shown in table 12. The second pair of market momentum exit/re-entry signals delivered by the Market Momentum System was not used because the FTSE 100 valuation triggers meant that the system was out of the market throughout this period.

Where sell and buy prices are shown in shaded cells, these indicate respectively occasions when the Market Momentum System triggered exits from and re-entries into the market. So, for example, there was a market momentum exit on 7 January 2008, even though the FTSE 100 value was still above 95%.

As you will see from the track record, there were three occasions when the Market Momentum System came into play. The first two produced capital losses because the re-entry price was higher than the exit price. The third occasion, during the credit crunch, produced a large capital gain since the re-entry price was less than 72% of the exit price.

In constructing this track record, I have replicated as closely as possible the actual costs and benefits which would be incurred by the accumulating fund. FTSE 250 investment is assumed to be undertaken via the i-Shares FTSE 250 UCITS ETF, which was recommended in Strategy 2, with dividends being automatically reinvested by your broker. Although this ETF has only been available for the last few years, I have replicated its cost structure across the whole period of FTSE 250 investment in this strategy.

The overall compound actual annual return for this strategy from the start of 1986 to 30 September 2014 has been 12.2%. This is a very strong result, outperforming the vast majority of commercial UK equity funds. Since annual inflation over this period averaged 3.47%, the annual real return has been 8.4%.

The development of the track record follows this pattern:

- The accumulated value of the initial investment, in the final column, shows the value of the fund when cash has been invested in the FTSE 250 ETF or when the ETF has been sold.

- Interest earned on cash is shown in the penultimate column.

- When the ETF position is sold, this creates a capital gain (or loss) from the difference between the selling price and the buying price. The typical buy/sell price spread for this ETF has also been taken into account.

- To this capital profit (or loss) has been added the extra value created by reinvested dividends, net of the effective costs charged by the ETF.

- The net capital profit (or loss) plus the value of reinvested dividends creates a total ETF value which is invested in cash when the ETF position is sold.

- Detailed assumptions are given after the table.

TABLE 12. LONG-TERM TRACK RECORD OF STRATEGY 4

Buy date	Sell date	% capital gain less spread	Capital gain less trans. costs	Fund value before reinvested divs	Value of reinvested divs net of fund costs	Net interest	Acc. fund (£)
01/01/86 (Fund Start)							10,000
						1315	11,315
28/10/87 (1915.6)	11/07/89 (2643.4)	37.9	4265	15580	614		16,193
						1083	17,277
09/04/90 (2417.7)	26/04/90 (2339.6)	-3.3	-593	16684	23		16,707
						1631	18,338
08/04/91 (2562.9)	24/12/93 (3773.2)	47.1	8619	26956	2225		29,181
						1331	30,512
07/03/95 (3327.9)	12/10/95 (3936.4)	18.2	5532	36044	451		36,495
						12000	48,494
11/07/02 (5065.1)	24/09/02 (4304.8)	-15.1	-7329	41165	255		41,421
						766	42,187
27/06/03 (4958.7)	23/01/07 (11102.2)	123.8	52185	94372	6899		101,271
						2235	103,506
16/08/07 (10462.6)	05/10/07 (11390.4)	8.8	9086	112592	698		113,290
						589	113,879
19/11/07 (10404.5)	07/01/08 (10093.1)	-3.1	-3183	100323	251		110,947
						3772	114,719
18/06/09 (7241.7)	30/09/14 (15379.7)	112.2	128746	243465	29678		273,144
		Compound annual return 1/1/86 to 30/09/14					12.19%

Assumptions

- FTSE 250 closing prices are used for each buy/sell date.

- The price shown for 30/09/2014 is a hold price rather than a sale price since no sale signal occurred on this date.

- The buy/sell spread is assumed to be 0.6%, based on the current typical spread.

- Each buy/sell transaction costs £12.50.

- Effective fund costs, including tracking errors, are assumed to be 0.465% p.a.

- The percentage increase through reinvested dividends takes into account the prevailing dividend yields, the period of investment and a dividend reinvestment transaction cost of 1%.

- The net interest is based on the UK base rate less 0.5%, taxed at the UK basic rate of tax, and takes into account the period invested.

- The investor is a basic rate UK taxpayer with no capital gains tax liabilities in excess of the CGT threshold.

Future performance prospects

Historically this strategy has produced an annual return about 1% higher than the passive long-term FTSE 250 investment strategy described in Strategy 2 (excluding the market momentum add-on). I would therefore expect future returns to be about 1% higher annually, meaning a **7.7%** actual return or **4.9%** real return, assuming inflation of 2.7% annually.

CHAPTER 8. STRATEGY 5 – LONG-TERM FTSE 100 FINANCIAL SPREAD TRADING STRATEGY

In *How to Value Shares and Outperform the Market,* I outlined a potential financial spread trading strategy. However, I had not at that stage conducted research into the potential returns. I have now completed extensive research into these returns and the results are spectacular.[7]

Before explaining the strategy and its track record, I will explain how financial spread trading works.

What are financial spread trades?

Financial spread trades are available for a wide range of financial instruments (e.g. equities, currencies, bonds). A spread trade is an agreement between a client and a spread trade provider to exchange the difference between the opening and closing price of a trade at a future date. If a spread trade contract is held to maturity, the closing price will be the price of the underlying futures market. The way spread trades work is best shown by way of an example.

Financial spread trade example

A quarterly spread trade on the FTSE 100 is used in this example.

On 21 March 2014, the FTSE 100 price is 6557. I think that the FTSE 100 price is going to rise over the next few months.

I get a spread trade quote for the June 2014 FTSE 100 contract, expiring on 20 June 2014. The quote is 6506-6510. The higher price is the buy price and the

---

7 This strategy was previously featured in the *Investors Chronicle.*

lower price is the sell price. The difference between the two prices is the *spread*. The spread is the profit margin of the spread trade provider.

I decide to buy at £5 per point at the price of 6510.

Fast forward to 19 June 2014. The FTSE 100 cash price has risen to 6812. The current quote for the FTSE 100 June 2014 contract is now 6810-6814. I decide to sell my open trade at the price of 6810. So I realise a profit of £5 x (6810-6510) = £5 x 300 = £1500.

What is an equity future and how are the prices derived?

Financial equity spread trade prices are based on equity futures prices. An equity futures contract on a share/index is a contract to buy or sell the share/index at a specific future date at a price agreed at the time of the contract. The price of the equity future is derived from the price of the underlying share/index, adjusted for two factors:

1. The interest benefit that the buyer of the contract will receive from postponing the purchase of the equity from the contract date to the future exercise date (hence this benefit is added to the cash price of the equity to derive the futures price).

2. The loss which the buyer of the contract will suffer through not receiving any dividends payable between the contract date and the future exercise date (hence this loss will be deducted from the cash price of the equity to derive the futures price).

The following actual intra-day data from 27 October 2014 demonstrates how the pricing is calculated.

FTSE 100 QUARTERLY SPREAD TRADE EXPIRING 19 DECEMBER 2014

Days to expiry	53
FTSE 100 price	6352.5
Spread trade mid-price	6330
Points difference	22.5
FTSE 100 dividend yield	3.67%
Value of dividend lost	34 points (6352.5 * 3.67% * 53/365)
Implied value of interest gained	11.5 points (34 less 22.5)
Implied interest rate	1.25% (11.5*(365/53)*(100/6352.5))

The spread trade prices are set by the spread trading firm and therefore may vary slightly from the futures prices.

The advantages of financial spread trading

There are six main advantages:

1. Profits on spread trades are free of any tax (capital gains or income tax). On the other hand, you cannot offset any losses on spread trades against any chargeable capital gains tax from other investments.

2. There is no stamp duty payable on spread trades.

3. There is no commission. This is covered by the spread.

4. You do not have to cover your total exposure with the spread trade provider. This means you can earn interest on the balance of your exposure via an instant-access interest-bearing account. So, in the above example, your initial exposure was £5 x 6510 = £32,550.[8] But you may only have been required to provide an initial deposit of £5 x 23 (£115) to cover this exposure (£23 is the initial deposit requirement of the spread trading firm for each pound per point traded). You would, however, be required to provide immediate additional deposit cover for any losses incurred on your position.

5. The buy/sell spreads can be narrower than for other derivative trades.

6. There are no administration fees on spread trading.

The potential disadvantages of financial spread trading

1. The extra leverage provided by spread trades is a double-edged sword. Whilst leverage will magnify your profits, it will also magnify your losses. It is up to you to monitor your position and provide any additional deposits to cover your losses. If you fail to do so, your position will be closed out at your expense. It is therefore essential to have a disciplined exit strategy.

2. Without a disciplined strategy, you could lose all of, or even more than, your initial investment.

3. To follow the key risk control measures which I will describe, you need to monitor your position at least daily and you will need to execute up to two trades per quarter.

---

8   This is the equivalent of the FTSE 100 contract price dropping to 0.

4. Because of the leverage, spread trading can be very nerve-wracking, especially in fast-falling markets (assuming you have placed a trade on the market rising). You have to be able to hold your nerve and, for my strategy, ignore short-term setbacks. These setbacks will definitely occur because of the fluctuating pattern of share prices.

The key decision elements of financial spread trading

Assuming that you intend to follow a strategy buying and selling FTSE 100 spread trades, you have five key decisions to make:

1. When to buy.

2. When to sell.

3. How much you want to invest.

4. How many pounds per point movement in the contract price you want to invest. In relation to your total investment, this determines the gearing of your trade. The gearing is the multiple of profit (or loss) on your investment you make in relation to the price movement of the contract. So, for example, if your gearing is 7, you will make or lose 7% of your investment for every 1% movement in the contract price.

5. What level of stop-loss to set. This is the price the contract has to reach for your position to be automatically closed.

Getting each of these five key decisions right is essential for a successful spread trading strategy. The strategy which I will describe in the next section maximises your chances of success in each of these decisions.

The FTSE 100 spread trading strategy

Key success drivers for the strategy

The first key success driver of this strategy is the effectiveness of the buy and sell signals from the FTSE 100 Valuation System, reinforced by the market freefall exit risk protection mechanism from the Market Momentum System.

If you are going to take a geared position on the FTSE 100, so that rises and falls in the FTSE 100 price magnify your profit or loss, your best chance of success is to take that position when the FTSE 100 price is most likely to increase. Similarly, you should exit that position when the FTSE 100 price is most likely to fall.

The track record of the FTSE 100 Valuation System, combined with the market freefall strategy, is stellar. Since 1984, the average annual growth of the FTSE 100 has been 12.98% for the signalled FTSE 100 investment periods against an average annual loss of 1.08% when the System indicated that you should not be invested in the FTSE 100.

The other key success drivers for this strategy are to set the correct level of gearing and stop-loss levels to match your appetite for risk and reward. I will start with a strategy which uses gearing of 7 times and a stop-loss level of 27.5%. This means that your profit and losses are magnified 7 times and that your position is automatically closed out if your losses exceed 27.5% of your investment fund.

I have chosen the gearing multiple of 7 because this is approximately the maximum gearing which will not risk wiping out your whole investment, given the historic volatility of the FTSE 100 price.[9] I have chosen the stop-loss level of 27.5% to minimise the numbers of trades stopped out without reducing your investment excessively if a trade is stopped out.

If you set the stop-loss level at a higher percentage, fewer trades will be stopped but the short-term hit suffered by your investment fund will be greater when a trade is stopped out. Later I will introduce a tool which I have developed to help you choose your optimum gearing and stop-loss levels for this strategy.

Summary of the strategy (gearing multiple of 7 and 27.5% stop-loss)

1. Establish a cash fund in a high-interest, instant-access cash account.

2. When the FTSE 100 valuation reaches 105% (or is currently above 105% if you are starting the strategy) and the Market Momentum System indicates that the market is not in freefall, transfer 27.5% of your cash fund to a spread trading account to buy a quarterly FTSE 100 spread trading futures contract, which has at least two months to expiry. So, say your total fund is £5000, you would allocate £1375 to the purchase of this first contract. Buy sufficient pounds per point so that the gearing on your total fund (including the 72.5% still held in cash) is approximately 7 times the movement of the FTSE 100 spread trade contract price.

---

9 Without any stop-loss in place.

3. Set a stop-loss price so that any loss on your total fund, including cash, cannot exceed 27.5% (in this case you set the stop-loss so that the maximum loss is £1375).

4. Unless the trade is stopped out as a consequence of step 3, hold the position for two calendar months and then sell on the earlier of:

    •   the day when the valuation falls below 105%.

    •   the day before contract expiry.

5. If the FTSE 100 valuation remains above 105% on the day of contract expiry, buy a new contract following the same principles from step 2 onwards, but adjusting your cash fund for any profit or loss that has been made on the contract. So, for example, if your total fund was £5000 when you bought the contract and you made a profit of £1000 from the contract, your new fund would be £6000 (plus any accrued interest) and 27.5% of this, i.e. £1650, would be allocated to a potential maximum loss on your next spread trade contract.

6. If the trade has been stopped out or sold before contract expiry, wait until the contract expiry date before buying a new contract, following the above principles from step 2 onwards, as soon as the FTSE 100 valuation rises to at least 105%.

7. When, as a result of the FTSE 100 valuations, you do not hold a spread trade position, hold all of your cash in the instant-access cash account(s).

8. In times of market freefall (very rare), apply the detailed rules as described later in this chapter.

Do not worry if you are unsure about how to execute any of these steps. I provide a detailed explanation below.

Risk controls of this strategy

This strategy incorporates several key risk controls:

•   You buy and sell contracts using a FTSE 100 valuation system which has a proven track record.

•   You only buy a new contract when the valuation is at least 105%.

•   You sell a contract after two months if the valuation has fallen below 105%.

•   You exit your position if your loss exceeds 27.5% of your total fund and you do not buy a new contract until both the current contract has expired and the valuation is at least 105%.

- Using the Market Momentum System described in Chapter 3, you exit or do not enter the market when the freefall criteria are met, irrespective of the valuation.

- Once you have exited the market because of market freefall, you do not re-enter the market until both the market momentum re-entry criteria are met and the valuation is at least 105%.

Executing the strategy in detail (gearing multiple of 7 and 27.5% stop-loss)

The strategy employs quarterly spread trade FTSE 100 futures contracts expiring on the third Friday of March, June, September and December.

STEP 1

Decide the overall amount you wish to invest and place this in a competitive high-interest, instant-access cash account. When this fund exceeds £85,000, you should have multiple accounts up to the £85,000 FSCS (Financial Services Compensation Scheme) compensation limit to minimise your risk of default by the deposit-taker.

STEP 2

When the FTSE 100 valuation reaches 105% (or is currently above 105% if you are starting the strategy) and the market is not in freefall, transfer 27.5% of this fund to your spread trading account and buy a quarterly FTSE 100 spread trade futures contract (if the amount to transfer is in excess of your cash account's same-day transfer limit, you will need to transfer these funds in advance when the valuation is approaching 105%).

If you wish to maximise the interest you earn on your cash account and are prepared to make frequent cash transfers to your spread trading account, you could initially transfer a lower sum to your spread trading account and subsequently make additional cash transfers to cover any increased margin requirements. The minimum margin requirements required by spread trading firms are low but you also have to cover any accumulating losses on the contract. This potential bonus interest has not been taken into account in the track record for the strategy.

It is essential that you understand and comply with the margin requirements of your chosen spread trading firm to ensure that your position is not automatically closed out before the 27.5% loss level is reached, i.e. the point at which you would lose all that you are prepared to lose on that contract. You may need to maintain a small buffer on your account in addition to the cash required to cover any accumulating losses.

Buy sufficient pounds per point so that the gearing on your total fund (including the 72.5% held in cash) is approximately 7 times the movement of the FTSE 100 spread trade contract price. This means that, if the contract price changes by 1%, the value of your total fund will change by approximately 7%, up or down. The expiry date of the contract should be at least two calendar months away but, subject to this proviso, the shortest duration available from the quarterly spread trade range. So, for example, if the trade date were 11 February, you would buy the contract with a June expiry date. This is because the next quarterly expiry date, on the third Friday in March, is less than two months away.

Determine the pounds per point to invest through the following formula:

(7 x your total fund) ÷ contract buy price

So, for example, if your total fund, including the 72.5% retained on your instant-access cash account, is £5000 and the FTSE 100 contract buy price is 6000, the calculation of pounds per point is (7 x £5000) ÷ 6000 = £5.83.

Most spread trading firms will allow you to trade in pennies as well as pounds per point, but there will be a minimum trade size, e.g. £0.50 per point. Rounding the trade to the nearest pound will increase or reduce the gearing accordingly.

STEP 3

Place a stop-loss price on your contract so that your contract is sold when it falls to a price which will limit your loss to 27.5% of your overall fund (including the cash on your instant-access account). This stop-loss price is calculated as follows:

contract buy price - (27.5% of your overall fund ÷ £ per point)

So, for example, if your overall fund is £5000, you want to limit your maximum loss to 27.5% of this fund i.e. £1375. Assume you are trading £5.83 per point and the contract buy price is 6000. The stop-loss contract price would be calculated as follows: 6000 - (1375 ÷ 5.83) = 6000 - 235.85 = 5764.15. This would be rounded up to 5765. This stop-loss price is approximately 4% below the contract buy price. If the price falls to this level your contract will automatically be sold to limit your loss to 27.5% of your total investment fund.

In fast markets, spread trading firms will not guarantee to execute your chosen stop-loss price if you use a standard stop-loss. However, for a small fee (around £1 per point traded), you can place a guaranteed stop-loss, which will guarantee execution of your chosen stop-loss price. Guaranteed stop-loss costs have not been included in the track record of the strategy. Between 8am and 9am UK time trade prices can be volatile and your trade could be prematurely stopped. If you wish to avoid this risk, adjust your stop-losses overnight to 30%, if your contract is approaching the 27.5% stop-loss trigger, and then reinstate the 27.5% stop as soon after 9am as possible.

STEP 4

Unless the trade is stopped out, hold the position for two calendar months. So, if you bought a contract on 20 May, you would hold until 20 July or the first trading day thereafter. Then sell on the earlier of:

- the day when the valuation falls below 105% (when the valuation is falling close to 105%, you should monitor valuations daily so that you can sell your position as soon as the valuation falls below 105%).

- the day before contract expiry.

STEP 5

If the valuation remains above 105% on the day of contract expiry, buy a new contract following the same principles from step 2 onwards, but adjust your cash fund for any profit or loss that has been made on the contract plus interest earned.

So, for example, if your total fund were £5000 when you bought the first contract and you made a profit, including interest, of £1000 from the contract, your new fund would be £6000 and 27.5% of this, i.e. £1650, would be allocated to a potential maximum loss on your next spread trade contract. Your new fund value would also be used to determine the pounds per point to buy on the next contract.

STEP 6

If the trade has been stopped out or sold before contract expiry, wait until the contract expiry date before buying a new contract, following the above principles from step 2 onwards, if the FTSE 100 valuation is above 105%.

Try to buy and sell contracts near to, but before, the end of the London Stock Exchange UK Equity trading day (4.30pm UK time).

STEP 7

When, as a result of the FTSE 100 valuations, you do not hold a spread trade position, hold all of your cash in the instant-access cash account(s).

STEP 8

In times of market freefall (very rare), apply the detailed rules as described below.

WHEN THE MARKET IS IN FREEFALL

For the purposes of this strategy, a FTSE 100 freefall is defined as the point when the FTSE 100 closing price crashes more than 10% below the price at which the 100-day simple moving average of closing prices has fallen below the 200-day simple moving average of closing prices. These conditions happen very rarely and have occurred only three times since 1984 for the FTSE 100. Free information services such as Digital Look (www.digitallook.com) provide facilities to calculate and graph moving averages. More information on the freefall system is contained in Chapter 3 on the Market Momentum System.

When the market has fallen to the freefall point as described above, you need to take cover until the storm subsides. Sell any FTSE 100 spread trade position irrespective of the FTSE 100 valuation. Only take out a new FTSE 100 spread trade position when both:

- The 100-day moving average of the FTSE 100 has risen upwards above the 200-day moving average, *and*
- The FTSE 100 valuation is above 105%.

RISK WARNING

As I will show in the next section, the track record of this strategy is stellar. However, it involves high risk in the short term and is not for the fainthearted. You should take appropriate professional advice before following this strategy. Future performance may not reflect past performance.

This strategy is designed for long-term investment (at least five years), as high losses can be incurred in the short term. On three occasions since 1984, two stop-loss activations have occurred in succession. It would be little comfort to a risk-averse, short-term investor who bailed out after the second stop-loss activation (by which time their total fund will have fallen in value by nearly 48%), that the losses were more than recovered subsequently. You may also be fully invested in cash for a long period, if the FTSE 100 remains overpriced for a long period.

The gearing on the total investment which this strategy uses is 7 on the contract price movement. This means that any percentage price movement in the FTSE 100 spread trade contract will be magnified approximately 7 times in your total investment, up or down. It only needs a fall in the contract sale price by 3.93% compared with your contract buy price for the trade to be stopped out and the loss on your total investment, excluding interest, to be 27.5%. That is why quite a few trades in the track record have been stopped out; on the other hand, the gains on the profitable trades have been correspondingly magnified.

You should fully familiarise yourself with the procedures and policies operated by your chosen spread trading firm before taking out any spread trade contracts. You are also exposed to risk of default by your spread trading firm. You should therefore be alert for any danger signs regarding the viability of the firm and, when your positions become sizeable, you may wish to spread your positions around a number of firms.

Track record of the strategy (gearing multiple of 7 and stop-loss of 27.5%)

The track record of the strategy is stunning. The compound annual returns, including interest after the basic rate of UK tax, have been up to 30 September 2014:

Since the start of 1984	26.15%
Last ten years	39.77%

£1000 invested at the start of 1984 would have grown to £1.27 million, free of any capital gains tax, by 30 September 2014.

No commercial UK equity fund has come close to this performance.

As I will show in the next section, even higher returns would be achieved by increasing the stop-loss levels. This of course would also increase the risk – a classic risk/reward equation.

The detailed track record of this strategy is shown in table 13.

TABLE 13. STRATEGY 5, LONG-TERM SPREAD TRADING TRACK RECORD. GEARING MULTIPLE OF 7 ON CONTRACT PRICE MOVEMENT, 27.5% STOP-LOSS, WITH MARKET FREEFALL EXIT AND RE-ENTRY USING SIGNALS FROM 100 AND 200 DAY MOVING AVERAGES

Invest. start date	End of day FTSE 100 price	Invest. exit date	End of day FTSE 100 price	Post-tax avg. interest rate %	Trade profit* %	Interest	Trade profit	Fund value at exit date
								1,000
01/01/84		27/06/85		7.38		110		1,110
27/06/85	1234.3	27/08/85	1310.8	7.71	34.95	10	388	1,508
27/08/85		23/09/85		7.40		8		1,516
23/09/85	1292.1	25/11/85	1455.5	7.75	80.29	15	1217	2,748
25/11/85		28/10/87		7.32		387		3,135
28/10/87	1658.4	09/11/87	1565.2	7.23	-27.50	5	-862	2,278
09/11/87		24/03/88		5.95		51		2,329
24/03/88	1782.7	10/06/88	1849.8	6.11	19.33	22	450	2,801
10/06/88		17/06/88		6.24		3		2,805
17/06/88	1850.1	25/08/88	1780.2	7.31	-27.50	28	-771	2,061
25/08/88		16/09/88		8.16		10		2,072
16/09/88	1766.7	15/12/88	1763.2	8.25	-12.20	31	-253	1,849
16/12/88	1773.9	16/02/89	2033.8	8.34	93.60	19	1731	3,599
16/02/89		23/04/90		9.49		403		4,003
23/04/90	2159.2	25/06/90	2398.5	10.00	64.96	50	2600	6,653
25/06/90		21/09/90		9.72		156		6,809
21/09/90	2025.5	20/12/90	2158.8	9.00	32.48	110	2212	9,130
21/12/90	2164.4	14/01/91	2080.8	9.18	-27.50	40	-2511	6,659
14/01/91		15/03/91		8.22		90		6,749
15/03/91	2494.2	06/06/91	2525.3	7.70	-1.08	86	-73	6,762
06/06/91		21/06/91		7.54		21		6,783
21/06/91	2487.5	21/08/91	2601.9	7.42	25.20	61	1709	8,553
21/08/91		20/09/91		7.18		50		8,604
20/09/91	2600.3	18/11/91	2502.9	7.09	-27.50	71	-2366	6,309
18/11/91		20/12/91		7.26		40		6,349

Invest. start date	End of day FTSE 100 price	Invest. exit date	End of day FTSE 100 price	Post-tax avg. interest rate %	Trade profit* %	Interest	Trade profit	Fund value at exit date
20/12/91	2358.1	19/03/92	2467.7	7.40	23.45	84	1489	7,922
20/03/92	2456.6	20/05/92	2711.9	7.40	65.67	71	5203	13,196
20/05/92		18/06/92		6.76		71		13,267
18/06/92	2584.8	02/07/92	2476.2	6.38	-27.50	24	-3648	9,642
02/07/92		18/09/92		6.58		136		9,777
18/09/92	2567.0	05/10/92	2446.3	6.17	-27.50	20	-2689	7,109
05/10/92		18/12/92		5.40		78		7,187
18/12/92	2789.7	18/02/93	2837.7	4.49	8.69	40	625	7,851
18/02/93		06/04/93		4.15		42		7,893
06/04/93	2832.2	07/06/93	2844.8	4.21	0.82	41	65	7,999
07/06/93		02/07/93		4.16		23		8,021
02/07/93	2857.7	02/09/93	3072.6	4.07	50.30	40	4035	12,096
02/09/93		08/03/95		4.76		870		12,966
08/03/95	2992.1	09/05/95	3261.2	5.48	58.52	88	7588	20,642
09/05/95		18/07/03		4.91		8,309		28,950
18/07/03	4073.2	18/09/03	4314.7	3.20	40.74	114	11794	40,859
19/09/03	4257.0	30/09/03	4091.3	3.11	-27.50	28	-11236	29,651
30/09/03		19/12/03		3.11		279		29,929
19/12/03	4412.3	19/02/04	4515.6	3.28	14.72	121	4406	34,455
19/02/04		19/03/04		3.37		92		34,548
19/03/04	4417.7	19/05/04	4471.8	3.60	6.65	151	2297	36,996
19/05/04		01/07/04		3.82		166		37,162
01/07/04	4424.7	16/09/04	4556.5	3.81	17.84	217	6630	44,009
17/09/04	4591.0	17/11/04	4796.9	3.70	28.73	197	12644	56,850
17/11/04		17/12/04		3.62		169		57,019
17/12/04	4696.8	17/02/05	5057.4	3.56	51.39	250	29302	86,571
17/02/05		31/03/05		3.66		365		86,935
31/03/05	4894.4	16/06/05	5045.0	3.80	18.51	505	16092	103,532
17/06/05	5077.6	15/09/05	5383.5	3.49	39.25	646	40636	144,815

Invest. start date	End of day FTSE 100 price	Invest. exit date	End of day FTSE 100 price	Post-tax avg. interest rate %	Trade profit* %	Interest	Trade profit	Fund value at exit date
16/09/05	5407.9	19/10/05	5167.9	3.42	-27.50	325	-39824	105,315
19/10/05		17/05/06		3.58		2,169		107,484
17/05/06	5675.5	26/07/06	5877.1	3.76	22.20	562	23862	131,908
26/07/06		15/09/06		3.89		717		132,625
15/09/06	5822.2	15/11/06	6160.3	3.67	41.23	590	54681	187,896
15/11/06		16/08/07		4.00		5,642		193,538
16/08/07	5859.9	16/10/07	6614.3	4.51	86.23	1,058	166888	361,483
16/10/07		15/01/08		3.98		3,587		365,070
15/01/08	6025.6	21/01/08	5578.2	3.62	-27.50	158	-100394	264,833
21/01/08		28/07/09		2.12		8,522		273,355
28/07/09	4528.8	17/12/09	5217.6	0.48	117.50	370	321192	594,917
18/12/09	5196.8	18/03/10	5642.6	0.52	64.71	553	384971	980,441
19/03/10	5650.1	04/05/10	5411.1	0.55	-27.50	494	-269621	711,315
04/05/10		18/06/10		0.52		460		711,774
18/06/10	5250.8	25/06/10	5046.7	0.50	-27.50	49	-195738	516,086
25/06/10		17/09/10		0.50		594		516,680
17/09/10	5508.0	16/12/10	5881.7	0.50	51.70	462	267123	784,265
17/12/10	5871.8	17/02/11	6087.4	0.62	27.98	599	219437	1,004,301
17/02/11		18/03/11		0.70		559		1,004,859
18/03/11	5718.1	16/06/11	5698.8	0.59	0.98	1,056	9848	1,015,763
17/06/11	5714.9	04/08/11	5393.1	0.59	-27.50	571	-279335	737,000
04/08/11		16/09/11		0.53		460		737,460
16/09/11	5368.4	22/09/11	5041.6	0.50	-27.50	44	-202801	534,702
22/09/11		16/12/11		0.50		623		535,325
16/12/11	5387.3	15/03/12	5940.7	0.50	77.60	478	415412	951,216
16/03/12	5965.6	05/04/12	5723.7	0.36	-27.50	136	-261584	689,767
05/04/12		15/06/12		2.00		2,683		692,451
15/06/12	5478.8	20/09/12	5854.6	2.00	54.55	2,668	377732	1,072,851
21/09/12	5852.6	20/12/12	5958.3	2.00	18.08	3,836	193971	1,270,658

Invest. start date	End of day FTSE 100 price	Invest. exit date	End of day FTSE 100 price	Post-tax avg. interest rate %	Trade profit* %	Interest	Trade profit	Fund value at exit date
20/11/12		21/12/12		2.00		2,158		1,272,817
21/12/12	5940.0	14/03/13	6529.4	1.50	74.78	3,148	951812	2,227,777
15/03/13	6496.0	05/04/13	6249.8	1.20	-27.50	1,115	-612639	1,616,253
05/04/13		21/06/13		1.20		4,092		1,620,345
21/06/13	6116.2	19/09/13	6625.4	1.20	55.02	3,476	891514	2,515,335
20/09/13	6596.4	08/10/13	6365.8	1.00	-27.50	899	-691717	1,824,517
08/10/13		20/12/13		1.00		2,646		1,827,162
20/12/13	6606.6	20/03/14	6542.4	1.00	-0.24	3,266	-4385	1,826,044
21/03/14	6557.2	19/06/14	6808.1	1.00	31.85	3,264	581595	2,410,903
20/06/14	6825.2	08/08/14	6567.4	1.00	-27.50	2,347	-662998	1,750,251
08/08/14		19/09/14		1.00		1,460		1,751,711
19/09/14	6837.9	30/09/14	6622.7	1.00	-27.50	383	-481721	1,270,373
Compound annual return from 16/09/04 to 30/09/14:								39.77%
Compound annual return from 1/1/84 to 30/09/14:								26.15%

* On total fund including cash

Notes on the track record

- Profits on the spread trades have been calculated from spread trade FTSE 100 buy and sell futures contract prices. Where historical spread trading prices are not available, the contract prices have been calculated from the factors which determine these prices: namely, FTSE 100 cash price, FTSE 100 dividend yield, short-term gilt rates, buy/sell spread and the number of days to the expiry of the contract. The calculated contract buy and sell prices may not exactly match the actual prices, but any difference is unlikely to have a material impact on the track record of this strategy. Prices from March 2013 are actual contract prices.

- *Investment exits* are either the sale (including stop-loss sales) of a spread trade contract or the exit of a period of full cash investment to buy a spread trade contract.

- The fund values at investment exit dates are calculated by applying both the profits/losses of the last trade (if applicable) and accrued interest over the period to the previous fund value.

- In rows where no trade profit is shown, there was no spread trade contract in place and all the fund was invested in cash.

- FTSE 100 valuations use the default values of 10% risk premium and 2% for annual real dividend growth. Other factors which form part of the valuations are the FTSE 100 cash price, the FTSE 100 gross dividend yield (for periods when the tax credit on dividends could be reclaimed by institutions), Bank of England calculations from market expectations for average and end-period inflation rates for the coming five years, and the gross redemption yield on five-year UK gilts. All of this was explained earlier in relation to the Stock Market Valuation System.

- Average interest rates have been generally calculated from the one-year UK gilt rate, after the prevailing basic rate of UK tax. Between 9 May 1995 and 29 August 2003, the average interest rate has been calculated from the UK base rate less 0.5%, after the prevailing basic rate of UK tax. From 29 March 2012, interest rates used have been based on a prevailing competitive instant-access cash account rate, after the prevailing basic rate of UK tax.

- For each trading day, the closing price of the FTSE 100 has been used to calculate the FTSE 100 valuations, and the associated buy/sell triggers for this strategy. Except where positions have been stopped out, contract prices and the associated profits and losses have been calculated with reference to the FTSE 100 closing prices for each day. The lowest FTSE 100 prices of each trading day have been used to determine whether a contract price reaches the appropriate stop-loss level and is stopped out before the expiry of the contract.

- Whilst every effort has been made to ensure the accuracy of the calculations, the Author and Publisher take no responsibility for errors or omissions as, among other factors, these calculations use data supplied by third parties.

- The strategy uses the buy-sell spreads, margin requirements and FTSE 100 quarterly spread trade futures contracts available from City Index/Barclays Stockbrokers.

- The business terms of spread trading firms and tax rules may change in the future in ways which could adversely affect the future results of these strategies.

Optimising gearing multiples and stop-loss levels

Whilst stop-loss levels limit the amount which you can lose on a single trade, they also limit the profit which you might have made on the trade had you waited until the normal exit date of the contract. By normal exit date I mean the point when you would have sold the contract under the strategy rules had the stop-loss not intervened. There are three situations in which you would sell under the normal strategy rules:

1. When, after holding the contract for two months or more, the FTSE 100 valuation falls below 105%.

2. The day before contract expiry, if the FTSE 100 valuation has not fallen below 105%.

3. When the criteria for a market freefall exit occur (very rare).

On the strategy track record which we saw in the previous section, there were 18 stop-loss triggered exits. On ten of these occasions, the loss would have been lower at the normal exit from the contract, had the stop-loss not intervened. Indeed, on several occasions, the loss would have turned into a healthy profit.

Since 1984 there have been 55 spread trades, of which only 13 were unprofitable at the point of normal exit. The average ungeared profit on each trade, including the loss-making trades, at the point of normal exit was 3.59%. So on a gearing of 7, the average trade profit at point of normal exit was 25.13% (7 x 3.59) of the investment fund. The highest ungeared loss on a trade at point of normal sale was 10.53%, or 73.71% on a gearing of 7 of the investment fund.

The highest interim loss, before the normal point of exit, has been 13.34% ungeared. This takes into account the lowest FTSE 100 prices achieved each day. In view of the fact that most stop-loss triggers reduce the eventual profit which could have been achieved, one possible strategy is to set the stop-loss percentage so high that no stop-losses are triggered. Sticking to whole numbers, that means a maximum gearing of 7 since a gearing of 8 would historically have resulted in an interim loss of over 100% of your investment fund (8 x 13.34 = 106.7%). Historically, a gearing of 7 would have resulted in a maximum interim loss of 93.4% (7 x 13.34%). So a stop-loss of 95% would have prevented any stop-losses being triggered.

Using a gearing multiple of 7 and a stop-loss percentage of 95% would have delivered the maximum return from this strategy.

From the start of 1984 to 18 September 2014 this means a **compound annual return of 36.91%**. At this rate an initial £1000 investment would have grown in that period to over £15 million.

This is of course a staggering result and does not take into account any constraints which spread trading firms might impose for investments growing to this size. You can test this result in the simulation tool which I discuss below.

Before you rush to follow this strategy using a gearing multiple of 7 and a stop-loss percentage of 95%, you should be aware that it is extremely high risk in the short term because:

- There is no guarantee that, in future, the highest ungeared interim loss will not exceed 13.34% – this might result in the stop-loss of 95% being triggered and the consequent loss of 95% of your fund.

- There is also no guarantee that, in future, the highest ungeared normal trade exit loss will not exceed 10.53%. With a gearing of 7, this could result in a trade exit loss exceeding the 73.71% suffered historically by this strategy.

That said, historically there has been no five-year period since 1984 when the capital value of the accumulated fund has not increased, even without taking into account reinvested interest.

FTSE 100 spread trading strategy simulation tool

To help you determine the best combination of gearing and stop-loss levels, according to your appetite for risk, I have developed a simulation tool to test the impact of differing levels of gearing and stop-loss over the last 30 years. You can download this tool from:

www.sharemaestro.co.uk/ShareMaestroFTSE100SpreadTradeStrategy.shtml

You will need Excel version 2003 or later to use the tool.

Example of using the tool for gearing and stop-loss levels of 7 and 95% respectively

Figure 15 below shows the tool being used to test the extreme gearing and stop-loss combination described in the previous section. You can see:

- The latest accumulated fund value, at the date specified, from an initial investment of £1000 on 1 January 1984.

- The compound annual percentage gain since 1984 and for the last 10 years.

- The change in fund values between any investment exit dates (columns C and O).

- The capital gains/losses on every trade (in the tool you can scroll up and down to see these).

Growth of the fund

The growth of the fund comes from two sources:

1. Percentage profits (losses) on each trade.

2. Interest uplift.

The trade profits and losses produce accumulated capital growth, as shown in figure 15. Interest is earned on the full fund between trades. It is also earned during trades on the part of the fund retained in the interest-earning cash account, i.e. the amount not required to cover the stop-loss.

The accumulated interest produces a percentage uplift to the accumulated capital growth. This percentage uplift will increase over time, as more interest is earned. The percentage interest uplift, once earned, will never reduce. However, any trade losses will reduce the capital sum to which the interest uplift is applied.

FIGURE 15. FTSE 100 SPREAD TRADING STRATEGY SIMULATION TOOL

	A	C	G	H	I	J	K	L	N	O
1	SHAREMAESTRO FTSE 100 SPREAD TRADING STRATEGY SIMULATION TOOL									
2			Normal		Normal			GEARING		STOP LOSS
3		Normal	Trade		Trade				7	-95
4		Trade	Exit *	Max %	Exit *	Max %				
5	Investment	Investment	Trade	Interim	Trade	Interim	Trade			FUND
6	Start	Exit	Profit %	Loss	Profit %	Loss	Profit	Trade		VALUE at
7	Date	Date	no gearing	no gearing	gearing	gearing	%	Profit £	Interest	exit date £
84	17/06/2011	15/09/2011	-6.10	-12.44	-42.70	-87.08	-42.70	-2,821,024	481	3,786,070
86	16/09/2011	15/12/2011	1.27	-9.29	8.89	-65.03	8.89	336,582	233	4,122,885
88	16/12/2011	15/03/2012	11.09	-0.90	77.60	-6.27	77.60	3,199,359	254	7,322,499
89	16/03/2012ˋ	14/06/2012	-7.77	-11.87	-54.39	-83.09	-54.39	-3,982,707	325	3,340,117
91	15/06/2012	20/09/2012	7.79	-0.77	54.55	-5.39	54.55	1,822,034	888	5,163,038
92	21/09/2012	20/12/2012	2.58	-3.80	18.08	-26.60	18.08	933,477	1,273	6,097,788
94	21/12/2012	14/03/2013	10.68	-1.13	74.78	-7.91	74.78	4,559,926	1,040	10,658,754
95	15/03/2013	20/06/2013	-4.28	-5.40	-29.96	-37.80	-29.96	-3,193,363	1,700	7,467,091
97	21/06/2013	19/09/2013	7.86	-1.52	55.02	-10.64	55.02	4,108,393	1,105	11,576,589
98	20/09/2013	19/12/2013	-0.05	-4.23	-0.35	-29.61	-0.35	-40,518	1,427	11,537,498
100	20/12/2013	20/03/2014	-0.03	-2.90	-0.24	-20.30	-0.24	-27,459	1,422	11,511,462
101	21/03/2014	19/06/2014	4.55	-0.88	31.85	-6.16	31.85	3,666,401	1,419	15,179,281
102	20/06/2014	18/09/2014	0.39	-4.15	2.73	-29.05	2.73	414,394	1,871	15,595,547
103	* without stop-loss being invoked prior to this date									
104	Dates shown in bold are market freefall exits and re-entry dates									
105										
106					Initial investment **		-1,000	01/01/1984		
107					Current capital value inc interest		15,595,547	18/09/2014		
108					Compound Annual Gain %		36.91			
109										
110					Fund value 10 years ago **		-145,477	16/09/2004		
111					Current fund value		15,595,547	18/09/2014		
112					Compound Annual Gain %		59.51			
113					** shown as a negative to calculate the compound annual gain%					

The data in the various columns is explained as follows:

A. Investment Start Date: The date when a trade is opened or a period of full cash investment starts.

C. Normal Trade Investment Exit Date: The normal trade exit date.

G. Normal Trade Exit Trade Profit % no gearing: The percentage trade profit, without gearing, on the normal trade exit date, without a stop-loss intervening.

H. Max % Interim Loss no gearing: The maximum percentage trade loss, without gearing, arising before the normal trade exit date.

I. Normal Trade Exit Trade Profit % gearing: The figure in column G, multiplied by the gearing multiple in cell L3.

J. Max % Interim Loss gearing: The figure in column H, multiplied by the gearing multiple in cell L3.

K. Trade Profit %: The geared trade profit percentage at normal trade exit date, unless the stop-loss has intervened, in which case this column shows the stop-loss percentage.

L. Trade Profit: The trade profit (or loss) calculated by applying the trade profit percentage in column K to the previous accumulated fund value shown in column O. This shows as zero when there is no spread trade in place.

N. Interest: Interest earned for the period of the investment.

O. FUND VALUE at exit date: The fund value at the investment exit date shown in column C. This value is obtained by applying interest earned and any trade profit/loss for the current investment period to the previous fund value.

The Compound Annual Gain % is calculated by Excel from the starting fund value and the closing fund value and their respective dates. The starting fund value is treated as an outflow and is therefore shown as a negative number.

Using the simulator to test the impact of different gearing and stop-loss levels

To use the simulation tool, you simply enter:

- Your chosen gearing level in cell L3.

- Your chosen stop-loss percentage in cell O3. *This must be entered as a negative number.*

Preventing stop-losses at different gearing levels

As discussed above, one high-risk, high-reward combination has historically been to set the stop-loss level high enough so that it is never invoked and that all trades proceed to their normal exit date. The lower the gearing, the lower the required stop-loss percentage needs to be. Each stop-loss level has been set by multiplying the highest interim trade loss percentage for this strategy since the start of 1984 (13.34%) by the chosen gearing. So, for example, multiplying 13.34 x 6 comes to just over 80. This results in the stop-loss level of 81% for a gearing of 6.

The results are shown in table 14 for an initial investment of £1000 at the start of 1984, including the accumulated interest. The results are spectacular. Even a gearing of 2, with stop-loss level of 27%, would have achieved an annual actual return of 16.56%. This is considerably higher than the long-term annual return achieved by the legendary Invesco Perpetual High Income fund.

TABLE 14: RESULTS OF APPLYING THE HIGHEST NECESSARY STOP-LOSS FOR EACH GEARING LEVEL

Gearing	Stop-loss %	Accumulated fund (£)	Annual actual return %
7	95	15,595,547	36.91
6	81	8,834,485	34.40
5	67	3,952,701	30.93
4	54	1,444,155	26.71
3	41	438,401	21.89
2	27	111,076	16.56

Trying other combinations of gearing and stop-loss levels

You can use the simulation tool to try out different combinations of gearing and stop-loss levels. In general, lower gearing and lower stop-loss levels involve less risk but also less reward. The returns shown in table 15 from the simulation tool are the returns which historically you would have achieved for an investment of £1000 at the start of 1984 to 18 September 2014. The table shows a selection of possible combinations using the simulation tool. All these deliver much higher returns than passive investment in the FTSE 100 (Strategy 1). Another way of using the simulator is to set the stop-loss level (i.e. the maximum loss on each trade) which matches your risk appetite and then vary the gearing level to determine the level which historically would have delivered the highest return.

TABLE 15. STRATEGY 5, LONG-TERM RESULTS FROM VARIOUS COMBINATIONS OF GEARING AND STOP-LOSS LEVELS

Gearing	Stop-loss %	Accumulated fund (£)	Annual actual return %
7	20	63,938	14.49
7	15	135,961	17.33
7	7	71,323	14.89
6	20	142,297	17.51
6	15	61,393	14.34
5	20	555,881	22.83
5	15	97,384	16.06
4	20	404,608	21.57
4	15	261,313	19.85
3	20	195,554	18.71
3	15	162,859	18.02
2	20	81,889	15.41
2	15	56,745	14.04

When using the tool, you should look not just at the final accumulated fund and the associated return, but also at the fluctuations in the fund values over the period. This will give you an idea of the nature of the rollercoaster ride. You can also see how the fund values would have changed over successive five-year periods by referring to the data in columns C and O.

Setting different gearing and stop-loss levels

Gearing level

Substitute your chosen gearing multiple in place of 7 in step 4 of the detailed strategy given earlier in this chapter. Determine the pounds per point to invest through the following formula:

(gearing multiple x your total fund) ÷ contract buy price

Say you want to use a gearing multiple of 5. If your total fund, including the amount retained on your instant-access cash account, is £5000 and the FTSE 100 contract buy price is 6000, the calculation of pound per point is (5 x £5000) ÷ 6000 = £4.17.

Most spread trading firms will allow you to trade in pennies as well as pounds per point but there will be a minimum trade size, e.g. £0.50p per point. Rounding the trade to the nearest pound will increase or reduce the gearing accordingly.

Stop-loss level

Substitute your chosen stop-loss percentage in place of 27.5% in step 5 of the detailed strategy given earlier in this chapter. The stop-loss price is calculated as follows:

> contract buy price – (chosen stop-loss percentage of your overall fund ÷ £ per point)

Say you want to use a stop-loss percentage of 20%. If your overall fund is £5000, this means that you want to limit your loss to 20% of £5000 = £1000. Assume you are trading £4.17 per point and the contract buy price is 6000. The stop-loss contract sale price would be calculated as follows: 6000 - (1000 ÷ 4.17) = 5760.2. This is then rounded to the nearest whole number.

CHAPTER 9. STRATEGY 6 – LONG-TERM FTSE 250 SPREAD TRADING STRATEGY

In Strategy 3, I explained the strategy for boosting returns from long-term investment in the FTSE 100 with market timing. In Strategy 4, I explained a similar strategy for the FTSE 250. The aim of both of those strategies was to maximise returns during periods of investment in the FTSE 100 and FTSE 250 respectively. It is the effectiveness of Strategy 3 that forms the backbone of the successful spread trading strategy which I detailed in Strategy 5. I will now examine applying the spread trading strategy to the FTSE 250.

The spread trading strategies employ quarterly spread trades. The average quarterly capital growth figures achieved by Strategies 3 and 4 *during periods of market investment* were:

- FTSE 100: 3.10%

- FTSE 250: 4.02%

The gearing from spread trading will magnify any capital growth. With a gearing multiple of, say, 7, and before taking into account the spread on each trade, the above growth figures would be magnified sevenfold to produce geared quarterly capital growth of:

- FTSE 100: 21.7%

- FTSE 250: 28.14%

However, the trade spreads on the FTSE 100 and the FTSE 250 differ because there is a much larger market in FTSE 100 trades. For example, the spreads currently offered by IG are approximately 0.06% for the FTSE 100 and 0.6% for the FTSE 250. Using again a gearing multiple of 7, those spreads would result in geared quarterly capital growth of:

- FTSE 100: 21.27%

- FTSE 250: 23.80%

So, even though the spread is ten times higher, the superior capital growth performance of the FTSE 250 should result in higher long-term performance for the spread trading strategy.

Very few spread trading firms offer quarterly contracts on the FTSE 250. Probably the most well-known is that offered by IG, which they call the FTSE Mid250. In addition to the spread being fairly wide, the margin requirements are also a lot higher than those of the FTSE 100. For example, currently, you need to place funds (known as margin) on your spread trading account equivalent to 5% of your total exposure for trades between 50p and £135 per point. These margin requirements are compatible with the strategy detailed below.

Executing the strategy in detail (gearing multiple of 7 and 27.5% stop-loss)

The strategy employs quarterly spread trade FTSE 250 futures contracts expiring in March, June, September and December.

Step 1

Decide the overall amount you wish to invest and place this in a competitive high-interest, instant-access cash account (when this fund exceeds £85,000, you should have multiple accounts up to the £85,000 FSCS compensation limit to minimise your risk of default by the deposit-taker).

Step 2

When the FTSE 100 valuation reaches 105% (or is currently above 105% if you are starting the strategy) and the market is not in freefall, transfer 27.5% of this fund to your spread trading account and buy a quarterly FTSE 250 spread trade futures contract (if the amount to transfer is in excess of your cash account's same-day transfer limit, you will need to transfer these funds in advance when the valuation is approaching 105%).

If you wish to maximise the interest you earn on your cash account and are prepared to make frequent cash transfers to your spread trading account, you could initially transfer a lower sum to your spread trading account and subsequently make cash transfers to cover any increased margin requirements. The minimum margin requirements required by spread trading firms are low but you also have to cover any accumulating losses on the contract.

Step 3

It is essential that you understand and comply with the margin requirements of your chosen spread trading firm to ensure that your position is not automatically closed out before the 27.5% loss level is reached. You may need to maintain a small buffer on your account in addition to the cash required to cover any accumulating losses.

Step 4

Buy sufficient pounds per point so that the gearing on your total fund (including the 72.5% held in cash) is approximately 7 times the movement of the FTSE 250 spread trade contract price. This means that, if the contract price changes by 1%, the value of your fund will change by approximately 7%, up or down. The expiry date of the contract should be the shortest duration available from the quarterly spread trading range, providing the expiry is at least two months away.

So, for example, if the trade date were 11 February, you would buy the contract with a June expiry date. This is because the nearest quarterly expiry date, on the third Friday in March, is less than two months away. Determine the pounds per point to invest through the following formula:

(7 x your total fund) ÷ contract buy price

So, for example, if your total fund, including the 72.5% retained on your instant-access cash account, is £5000 and the FTSE 250 contract buy price is 15000, the calculation of pounds per point is (7 x £5000) ÷ 15000 = £2.33.

Most spread trading firms will allow you to trade in pennies as well as pounds per point but there will be a minimum trade size, e.g. £0.50p per point. Rounding the trade to the nearest pound will increase or reduce the gearing accordingly.

Step 5

Place a stop-loss price on your contract so that your contract is sold at a price which will limit your loss to 27.5% of your overall fund (including the cash on your instant-access account). This stop-loss price is calculated as follows:

contract buy price – (27.5% of your overall fund ÷ £ per point)

So, for example, if your overall fund is £5000, you want to limit your maximum loss to 27.5% of this fund, i.e. £1375. Assume you are trading £2.33 per point and the contract buy price is 15000. The stop-loss contract price would be calculated as follows: 15000 - (1375 ÷ 2.33) = 14410.

Step 6

In fast markets, spread trading firms will not guarantee to execute your chosen stop-loss price if you use a standard stop-loss. However, for an extra spread of about 0.3%, you can place a guaranteed stop-loss, which will guarantee execution of your chosen stop-loss price. Due to their cost, guaranteed stop-losses will impact the long-term returns from this strategy. You may therefore wish to limit their use to times of market freefall when the 100 day moving average has already crossed downwards below the 200 day moving average.

Between 8am and 9am UK time trade prices can be volatile and your trade could be prematurely stopped. If you wish to avoid this risk, adjust your stop-losses overnight to 30% if your contract is approaching the 27.5% stop-loss trigger, and then reinstate the 27.5% stop as soon after 9am as possible.

Step 7

Unless the trade is stopped out, hold the position for two calendar months. So, if you bought a contract on 20 May, you would hold until 20 July or the first trading day thereafter. Then sell on the earlier of:

- The day when the valuation falls below 105% (when the valuation is falling close to 105%, you should monitor valuations daily so that you can sell your position as soon as the valuation falls below 105%).

- The day before contract expiry.

Step 8

If the valuation remains above 105% on the day of contract expiry, buy a new contract following the same principles from step 2 onwards but adjust your cash fund for any profit or loss that has been made on the contract. So, for example, if your total fund was £5000 when you bought the contract and you made a profit, including interest, of £1000 from the contract, your new fund would be £6000 and 27.5% of this, i.e. £1650, would be allocated to a potential maximum loss on your next spread trade contract.

Step 9

If the trade has been stopped out or sold before contract expiry, wait until the contract expiry date before buying a new contract, following the above principles from step 2 onwards, if the FTSE 100 valuation is above 105%.

Step 10

Try to buy and sell contracts near to, but before, the end of the London Stock Exchange UK Equity trading day (4.30pm UK time).

Step 11

When, as a result of the FTSE 100 valuations, you do not hold a spread trade position, hold all of your cash in the instant-access cash account(s).

Step 12

In times of market freefall (very rare), apply the detailed rules as described below.

When the market is in freefall

For the purposes of this strategy, a FTSE 250 freefall is defined as the point when the FTSE 250 closing price crashes more than 10% below the price at which the 100 day simple moving average of closing prices has crossed downwards below the 200 day simple moving average of closing prices. These conditions happen very rarely and have occurred only four times since 1984. Free information services such as Digital Look (www.digitallook.com) provide facilities to calculate and graph moving averages. See Chapter 3.

When the market has fallen to the freefall point, you need to take cover until the storm subsides. Sell any FTSE 250 spread trade position irrespective of the FTSE 250 valuation. Only take out a new FTSE 250 spread trade position when both:

- The FTSE 250 100-day moving average has risen upwards above the 200-day moving average, *and*
- The FTSE 100 valuation is above 105%.

Trade entry and exit dates

The trade entry and trade exit criteria are the same as for the FTSE 100 spread trading strategy, except that the market freefall risk control uses FTSE 250 moving averages (100 day and 200 day) instead of FTSE 100 moving averages.

Track record of the strategy

Although, as I have explained, the long-term returns from this strategy should be even higher than those of the FTSE 100 spread trading strategy, I do not have a detailed long-term track record which would identify the volatility and associated risks of FTSE 250 spread trading prices. I would therefore urge caution in the use of this strategy by, for example, limiting the gearing multiple to a maximum of 7 and stop-loss levels to a maximum of 27.5%.

Using different gearing multiples and stop-loss levels

You can apply your chosen gearing multiple and stop-loss level to this strategy in the same way as I detailed for Strategy 5.

CHAPTER 10. STRATEGY 7 – RUNNING A TAX-EFFICIENT FTSE 100 TRACKER THROUGH SPREAD TRADING

As I will explain in Part 3 on Practical Considerations, you should where possible operate Strategies 1 and 2 through a tax-free wrapper such as an ISA or a SIPP. However, it can be difficult to operate Strategies 3 and 4 through these wrappers, since the providers currently offer derisory interest rates for the periods when you will be out of the market.

Strategy 7 takes advantage of the tax-free nature of spread trading to provide a synthetic FTSE 100 tracker which should virtually match the performance of the FTSE 100 tracker provided through the normal ETF route.

So, while generally spread trading is associated with magnifying the risks and rewards of the underlying security, in this case the strategy matches the risks and rewards of the FTSE 100, but with the added bonus of tax relief. This strategy also avoids the administrative complexity of calculating and reporting dividends and any capital gains for tax returns. I will first explain the basic steps for creating the synthetic tracker and then I will compare its performance with that of a competitive FTSE 100 ETF tracker.

Unfortunately, the wider spreads operated for FTSE 250 spread trading make this strategy unsuitable for providing synthetic FTSE 250 trackers.

The basic steps to create the synthetic FTSE 100 tracker

This synthetic FTSE 100 tracker is intended for use in the FTSE 100 strategies, Strategies 1 and 3, instead of a FTSE 100 ETF. In all other respects these strategies remain the same when you are using the synthetic tracker following the steps below – you buy the tracker (by buying FTSE 100 spread trade contracts) and sell the tracker (by selling your spread trade contracts) when you would buy and sell the FTSE ETF according to these strategies.

1. Decide how much you want to invest in your tracker.

2. Deposit 90% of this amount on a competitive instant-access cash account.

3. Open a spread trading account with the remaining 10%.

4. Buy a quarterly FTSE 100 spread trade with sufficient pounds per point to provide exposure equivalent to the total amount of your investment. For example, if the FTSE 100 contract buy price were 6100 and your total investment (the 10% on your spread trading account plus the 90% on your instant-access cash account) were £18,000, you would invest £2.95 per point (18,000/6100).

5. Establish a stop-loss level 10% lower than the contract buy price. In this example: 6100 x 90% = 5490.

6. Monitor the contract price level. If the contract price is in danger of breaching the stop-loss limit, which should only happen very occasionally, transfer sufficient funds from your instant-access cash account to your spread trading account and increase the stop-loss level accordingly. It is essential that your trade is not stopped out if you are to track the performance of the FTSE 100.

7. On the day before contract expiry, towards the end of the trading day (4.30 pm UK time) sell your contract. Calculate your new total investment fund by applying the profit/loss on the sold trade plus interest accrued on the cash account to your total investment fund at the purchase date of the contract which you have just sold. Immediately open a new contract expiring at the end of the next quarter. Determine the pounds per point to invest in the new contract with reference to your new total investment fund and the buy price of the new contract. For example, if your new total investment fund were £18,590 and the new contract buy price were 6320, you would invest £2.94 per point (£18,590/6320).

Note: under the current spreads offered by spread trading firm IG, if the increase in the pound per point investment as a result of a trading profit were higher than the minimum pound investment per point, you could achieve a spread saving by rolling over the existing contract into the next quarter and buying a separate contract for the increased amount only. This saving arises because IG do not charge a spread on the sale contract of rolled over trades. Other spread trading firms offer reduced spreads for rolling over trades. You will need to consult your spread trading firm for the detailed procedures for rolling over trades.

8. Transfer funds between your instant-access cash account and your spread trading account to ensure that 90% of your cash (total investment fund) is in the instant-access cash account and 10% is in the spread trading account. Ensure that the initial stop-loss level on the new contract is equivalent to a 10% loss on your new total investment fund, as described in step 5 above.

9. Continue the cycle, repeating the above steps.

Financial comparison

In the following tables I give a detailed comparison of the synthetic spread trading FTSE 100 tracker with a conventional FTSE 100 ETF tracker. The comparison includes two quarters to show the impact of renewing the spread trading position for the second quarter. I have assumed the cost structure of the i-Shares ETF which I recommended in Strategy 1 and the current quarterly FTSE 100 spread trade contract terms offered by spread trading firm IG. I have assumed that the FTSE 100 price determining the sale price of the old contract and the buy price of the new contract will be the same. This will certainly be the case for contracts which are rolled over into the next quarter. Where you have to physically sell one contract and buy another, there will be a small time interval, during which period the FTSE 100 price may change. It may change in your favour or against you, but over time the changes may even out.

You will see that, for standard-rate UK taxpayers, who will have no capital gains tax liability as a result of selling all or part of their FTSE 100 tracker, there is little to choose financially between operating a synthetic FTSE 100 spread trading tracker and a standard FTSE 100 ETF tracker. However, higher rate UK taxpayers should benefit from not having to pay the higher rate tax on dividends through using the spread trading tracker. Similarly, those who are liable to pay capital gains tax on the whole of any gain (even at the current lower 18% band) should benefit from the synthetic spread trading tracker.

In the assumptions below, there are only four factors which affect the financial comparison:

1. The difference between the cash interest rate used to determine spread trading prices and the cash interest rates available to retail investors on instant-access cash accounts. I have used those rates which are typical at the time of writing. However, if you can obtain instant-access interest rates which are higher than those used to determine spread trading prices, you are likely to swing the financial comparison in favour of financial spread trading, even without the benefit of higher rate tax and capital gains tax savings.

2. The running costs of FTSE 100 ETFs.

3. The spreads charged by spread trading firms on quarterly FTSE 100 ETF contracts (i.e. the difference between the buying and selling prices). These can vary and so you are advised to compare several providers.

4. The buy/sell spread on the FTSE 100 ETF.

The FTSE 100 prices chosen for the opening and closing of each quarter do not affect the financial comparison.

Assumptions

To make the comparison easier to follow, I have assumed an initial total investment fund of £10,000. The other assumptions are shown in table 16. The results are shown in table 17.

TABLE 16. ASSUMPTIONS FOR COMPARISON BETWEEN AN ETF AND A SYNTHETIC SPREAD TRADE FTSE 100 TRACKER

FTSE 100 1st quarter opening level	6400
FTSE 100 1st quarter closing level	6500
FTSE 100 2nd quarter closing level	6600
Initial investment	10000
Annual FTSE 100 Dividend Yield net of UK basic rate %	3.5
Annual interest rate used for FTSE 100 quarterly spread contracts	1.25
Annual instant-access cash interest rate after basic rate UK tax	1.00
Proportion of synthetic fund maintained as instant-access cash	0.9
Annual ETF fund charge rate	0.46%
Buy/sell spread on FTSE 100 ETF %	0.03
Quarterly point spread charged on mid-point price for each trade	2

TABLE 17. RESULTS OF COMPARISON BETWEEN ETF AND SYNTHETIC SPREAD TRADE FTSE 100 TRACKER

ETF INVESTMENT	QUARTER 1
Initial investment post buy/sell spread	9997.00
Capital value at end of quarter before dividends and charges	10153.20
Reinvested dividends for quarter less 1% transaction fee	87.95
ETF value at end of quarter before charges	10241.16
(Less ETF charges)	-11.78
Capital value at end of quarter	10229.38

	QUARTER 2
Capital value at start of quarter	10229.38
Capital value at end of quarter before dividends and charges	10386.75
Reinvested dividends for quarter less 1% transaction fee	89.98
ETF value at end of quarter before charges	10476.73
(Less ETF charges)	-12.05
Capital value at end of quarter	10464.68

SYNTHETIC ETF INVESTMENT	QUARTER 1
Initial total investment	6400
Initial cash on deposit	9000.00
Initial cash on spread trading account	1000.00
Deemed value of dividends forgone in spread trade	56.00
Deemed interest benefit of spread trade position	20.00
Buying price of spread trade including spread	6366.00
Pounds per point investment in first quarter trade	1.57
Selling price of trade after deduction of spread	6498.00
Profit (loss) on spread trade	207.35
Interest on instant-access cash account less basic rate tax	22.50

Capital value at end of quarter	**10229.85**

Value of capital gains tax saving at 18% rate for the quarter	26.00
Value of capital gains tax saving at 28% rate for the quarter	40.44
Value of higher rate tax saving on dividends for the quarter	21.99
Higher rate tax on cash interest for the quarter	5.62

	QUARTER 2
Caital value at start of quarter	**10229.85**
Cash on deposit	9206.87
Cash on spread trading account	1022.99
Deemed value of dividends forgone in spread trade	56.88
Deemed interest benefit of spread trade position	20.31
Buying price of spread trade including spread	6465.44
Pounds per point invested in second quarter trade	1.58
Selling price of trade after deduction of spread	6598.00
Profit (loss) on spread trade	209.75
Interest on instant-access cash account less basic rate tax	23.02
Capital value at end of quarter	**10462.61**

Value of capital gains tax saving at 18% rate for the quarter	26.16
Value of capital gains tax saving at 28% rate for the quarter	40.69
Value of higher rate tax saving on dividends for the quarter	22.49
Higher rate tax on cash interest for the quarter	5.75

Accumulated value of capital gains tax saving at 18% rate	52.16
Accumulated value of capital gains tax saving at 28% rate	81.13
Accumulated value of higher rate tax saving on dividends	44.48
Accumulated cost of higher rate tax on cash interest	11.38

Conclusions

By the end of the second quarter, the projected value of the synthetic ETF is £10,462.61 compared with £10,464.68 for the actual ETF – a shortfall of just over 0.02%. This gap is very small and could easily be reversed by changes to the difference between the interest rate used to calculate spread trading prices and the interest rate available on a competitive instant-access account. However, the benefits of the synthetic ETF for those with higher rate tax or capital gains tax liabilities are clear-cut, providing you are prepared to follow the disciplined, systematic approach which the synthetic ETF strategy requires:

- By the end of the second quarter, the accumulated value of the higher rate tax saving on dividends is £44.48, or 0.44% of the starting investment value. Additional higher rate tax of £11.38 payable on interest received for the two quarters would need to be offset against this saving, if applicable.

- By the end of the second quarter, the accumulated potential value of the capital gains tax saving, at the 18% rate, is £52.1, or 0.52% of the starting investment value. At the 28% rate, the accumulated saving is £81.13, or 0.81% of the starting investment value. These savings take no account of any available annual tax-free capital gains tax allowance which the investor may have.

- These tax benefits far outweigh any shortfall of investment value for the synthetic ETF compared with the actual ETF and will continue to accumulate during the life of the strategy.

Notes on the calculations (in order of the fields)

Actual ETF investment

1. The actual ETF is assumed to be bought at the FTSE 100 price for the start of the quarter, less the buy/sell spread. The full spread has been used on the assumption that the investor will sell the ETF at some stage. No transaction fee has been included since this is assumed to be a long-term investment and these costs will become insignificant over time.

2. The ETF value at the end of the quarter, before reinvested dividends and charges, is calculated by changing the initial investment value pro-rata to the change in the FTSE 100 price over the quarter.

3. The value of reinvested dividends is calculated on the value of the ETF, before dividend reinvestment and charges, at the end of the quarter. The dividend yield is that given in the assumptions, pro-rated for the quarter.

4. ETF charges at the rate given in the assumptions, pro-rated for the quarter, are deducted from the above value to get the final ETF value at the end of the quarter.

5. In the second quarter, the capital value of the ETF at the end of this quarter, before dividend reinvestment, is calculated by adjusting the opening value of the ETF in relation to the change in the FTSE 100 price over the quarter. To this capital value dividends for the quarter are added and ETF costs for the quarter are deducted to get the closing value of the ETF at the end of the quarter.

Synthetic ETF investment

1. 90% of the initial investment is allocated to the interest-earning cash account and 10% to the spread trading account.

2. The deemed value of dividends foregone reduces the trade contract price and is calculated from the prevailing FTSE 100 dividend yield and price plus the number of days to contract expiry. This value reduces the contract price. At the beginning of Chapter 8 I explained how FTSE 100 quarterly spread trading prices are calculated.

3. The deemed interest benefit of investing in the trade contract is the avoidance of having to lay out cash to buy a long FTSE 100 ETF position. It is calculated from the prevailing FTSE 100 price, the prevailing short-term sterling interest rate and the number of days to contract expiry. This value increases the trade contract price.

4. The buying price of the spread trade contract is calculated by adding the spread points to the trade price, which is calculated by adjusting the FTSE 100 price for the loss of dividend income and for the benefit of interest saved.

5. The selling price of the spread trade contract at the end of the quarter is calculated by deducting the trade spread points from the prevailing FTSE 100 price. As there is minimal time to the expiry of the contract, no allowance is made for the loss of dividend income nor for the benefit of interest saved.

6. The profit (loss) on the trade for the quarter is calculated by deducting the buying price from the selling price and multiplying by the number of pounds per point invested in that trade.

7. Interest on the instant-access cash account is calculated by applying the assumed interest rate to the balance on this account at the start of the quarter.

8. The total capital value at the end of the quarter is calculated by adding the accrued interest and the profit (loss) to the initial investment value at the start of the quarter.

9. The capital gains tax saving for the quarter is calculated by applying 18% to the increase in value (if any) of the ETF over the quarter, less reinvested dividends. If a capital gains tax liability were to arise for a higher rate taxpayer, 28% would be used instead of 18%.

10. The higher rate tax saving on dividends is calculated by applying 25% to the accrued ETF dividends for the quarter.

11. The pounds per point invested in the second quarter trade are calculated from dividing the total capital value at the end of the previous quarter by the buy price of the FTSE 100 contract at the start of this quarter.

12. The values in the remaining fields for the second quarter are calculated in the same way as for the first quarter.

13. The final four rows give the accumulated value of the higher rate dividend tax and capital gains tax savings (at both the 18% and 28% rates) for both quarters, together with the accumulated cost of higher rate tax payable on the cash interest.

PART C.
PRACTICAL CONSIDERATIONS

INTRODUCTION

In addition to having the right investment strategies, it is essential that you have the right choice of investment vehicles and service providers to maximise your long-term returns. You should also avoid having your capital eaten up by income tax or capital gains tax. This means that you should maximise the use of tax-free wrappers (see below). Similarly, you should avoid heavy fees severely reducing your annual returns.

I will recommend service providers whom I have found to be relatively inexpensive and efficient. You should, however, conduct your own research because this is a very competitive market and charges change frequently. Where I quote fees, they are those applicable at the time of writing. When you are choosing a FTSE 100 or FTSE 250 tracker fund for Strategies 1 to 4, you need to take into account the following costs:

- The effective annual costs of the fund. Do not be misled by the annual charge quoted by the fund. From the fund website look at the difference over the last few years between the performance of the fund and the performance of the index which the fund is tracking. This difference will include any tracking error and all the fund costs, including those that are hidden.

- The annual administration fee charged by the service provider through which you purchase the fund. This is often a percentage of value (ad valorem) fee capped at a certain amount.

- Transaction charges for reinvesting dividends.

- As explained in Strategies 1 to 4, I currently recommend the use of ETFs for operating tracker funds and specifically the i-Shares FTSE UCITS 100 (code ISF) for the FTSE 100 and the i-Shares FTSE UCITS 250 (code MIDD) for the FTSE 250.

I would not worry too much about the transaction fees for purchasing and selling the funds (unless they are exorbitant) since these transactions will be very infrequent.

CHOOSING THE RIGHT INVESTMENT VEHICLE FOR EACH STRATEGY

In this section I cover the best investment vehicles for each strategy. I also recommend a reliable competitive service-provider for each investment vehicle. These recommendations are based on fees and service levels current at the time of writing. I have not included administration fees in the track records of strategies 1 to 4, because firstly they are quite small, if you choose an ETF and the right service provider, and secondly the impact on returns will vary tremendously according to the size of your funds.

Strategies 1 and 2 – Long-term investment in the FTSE 100 and FTSE 250

Where possible, you should use a tax-free investment vehicle such as an ISA (Individual Savings Account) or a SIPP (Self Invested Personal Pension). This will not incur capital gains tax and any higher rate tax on dividends.

I do not explain how these tax-free investment vehicles work because you can find detailed information on the websites of the service providers which I recommend.

These tax-free vehicles would also be suitable for the variations on these two strategies which use the Market Momentum System. On the rare occasions when you are out of the market through market momentum exit signals, you may suffer poor interest on your ISA or SIPP account but this should not have a material impact on the benefit of the Market Momentum Strategy.

For the FTSE 100 only, you could also employ as an investment vehicle a synthetic FTSE 100 fund through spread trading, as described in Chapter 10.

When you have used up your available tax-free investment allowances and you wish to make further investment in one of these strategies, a suitable vehicle would be a share account provided by an online broker.

Strategies 3 and 4 – Boosting long-term investment in the FTSE 100 and FTSE 250 with market timing

These strategies switch between ETF investment and cash according to market timing signals. Of the tax-free investment vehicles, SIPPs are currently not suitable because they pay minimal rates of interest on cash and, once you make a withdrawal from a SIPP, you lose the tax-free status of that money.

ISAs are potentially suitable investment vehicles because the new ISA regime (NISA) allows you to transfer both ways between stocks and shares ISAs and cash ISAs. However, in practice the ISA option is also ruled out because the transfers from an investment ISA to a cash ISA can take up to three weeks. If the transfer time is speeded up to same-day, the ISA option would be ruled in again.

Furthermore, when the era of artificially low base rates comes to an end, both ISAs and SIPPS may start paying reasonable rates of interest on cash and at this time ISAs and SIPPs may be viable for use with these strategies. You may also decide to use an ISA as an investment vehicle because the protection from capital gains tax for you more than compensates for low interest rates on cash.

For the FTSE 100 strategy only, you could employ as an investment vehicle a synthetic FTSE 100 fund through spread trading, as described in Chapter 10. The spread trading profits are tax-free. Tax is only payable on interest earned from the instant-access cash account.

You could use a share account from an online broker, outside a tax shelter, for both of these strategies. Even if you end up paying some capital gains tax as a result of ETF sales, you are likely to earn a better net of tax return than keeping your funds on cash deposit all the time. Higher rate taxpayers will also have to pay tax on dividends received from the ETF. In addition, tax will be payable on interest from the instant-access cash accounts which form part of both strategies (when you are out of the market).

Strategies 5 and 6 – Long-term FTSE 100 and FTSE 250 spread trading strategies

The investment vehicles for these strategies are spread trading accounts and instant-access cash accounts, for which I provide details below. The only tax payable will be on interest received from the instant-access cash accounts.

Strategy 7

See Chapter 10.

RECOMMENDED SERVICE PROVIDERS

All the recommended service providers offer online accounts, which I recommend that you use. You can open an account online and trade online very easily. I have chosen firms which, at the time of writing, have good customer service as they will help you with any problems. However, service levels and fees can change rapidly. You should therefore check, preferably online, the latest comparative fees, news and reviews before choosing a service provider.

Please do not think that operating an online investment account is difficult. It is extremely easy.

ISAs

I recommend Barclays Stockbrokers (www.barclaysstockbrokers.co.uk) for Stocks and Shares ISAs (also known as Investment ISAs). They charge a flat administration fee of £36 a year for ETFs, have a good online platform and generally provide good customer service. They provide automated dividend reinvestment for a 1% transaction fee, minimum £1 and maximum £7.50.

SIPPs

I also recommend Barclays Stockbrokers as a service provider for SIPPs, providing your fund is over £42,000 in size. There is a flat administration fee of £186 a year. There is also a range of other charges for the various actions which you may perform on your SIPP, e.g. £75 per transfer in. The fees are higher than for ISAs because of the extra complexity involved in SIPP administration, but Barclays' fees are competitive.

Hargreaves Lansdown (www.hl.co.uk) are also a good SIPP service-provider. They have very good customer service and no setup fee. Their ongoing administration fee is 0.45% of value (ad valorem), capped at £200 per year (reached at £44,444). There is also a range of charges for other SIPP actions.

Online Share account (non ISA)

I recommend Hargreaves Lansdown. They have a yearly ad valorem administration fee of 0.45%, capped at £45 per year. They also offer automatic dividend reinvestment for a flat transaction fee of £1.50 per dividend reinvested. They have a very good online platform and their customer service is also very good.

Instant-access cash account(s)

You can find the current best available rates from www.moneyfacts.co.uk. I recommend that you choose an institution with an online service which enables you to transfer money easily between this account and your share account. Ideally you should invest no more than £85,000 per banking licence. This is the FSCS compensation limit if the firm goes bust.

Spread trading firm

I recommend IG (www.ig.com/uk). They are the global leader in financial spread trading, which is also known as spread betting. I have found their customer service to be excellent and their online platform is very good, with good training should you need it. Their spreads are very narrow and the margin requirements are comparatively low. A tight spread is very important because it both improves your long-term returns and could prevent a trade being closed out prematurely because of a stop-loss.

There are of course plenty of other spread trading firms available. Whichever firm you choose, you should thoroughly acquaint yourself with their terms of business and their trading platform before committing to live trades. You should also monitor the health of the firm, since there is a limited compensation scheme for spread trading and you are at risk if the firm ceases trading.

TAX INFORMATION

Current tax rates and allowances are available from HMRC (www.hmrc.gov.uk). This site also provides information on how tax rates and allowances are applied. Tax planning is outside the scope of this book but effective tax planning, especially for families, can significantly reduce the impact of tax on your long-term savings. I covered some of these techniques in *How to Value Shares and Outperform the Market*.

Epilogue

I hope that this book inspires you to try at least one of the strategies which it covers. If some of the strategies seem a little complicated at first, please persevere. Your effort should be amply rewarded. Once you have understood the requirements to follow each strategy, the weekly effort needed to execute each strategy is small.

Some readers may still be concerned about the perceived risks of UK equity investment. They may believe that cash is safer. However, as I explained at the outset, cash is not a risk-free, long-term investment. If, as I believe, the critical success factor for long-term investment (five years upwards) is maximising real long-term returns, then cash fails miserably. Currently the best five-year cash deposit rate is projected to deliver a negative annual real return of -0.3%, after basic rate tax. In other words, your cash investment is likely to be worth less in real terms in five years time than it is now.

On the other hand, I project that, by following even the simplest strategies in this book (Strategies 1 and 2), you should achieve real long-term returns of at least 2.7% annually, after basic rate tax. The other strategies should deliver considerably higher returns than this, as they use my proven Market Valuation System and Market Momentum System for maximising returns and minimising risk.

Of course, unlike death and taxes, these higher returns are not guaranteed. Nevertheless, it is *probable* that each of the strategies will deliver much higher real long-term returns than cash. And as Cicero said, "Probability is the very guide of life."

I wish you every success in your journey to a secure financial future.

Appendix – Glossary Of Terms

Bonds

Companies or governments issue bonds when they wish to raise money. The bonds may have fixed or variable interest rates and some bonds are convertible into shares upon conditions set when the bond is issued.

After the primary sale of the bonds to raise money for the issuing institution, bonds, being securities, are tradable on the secondary market. UK government bonds are called Gilts.

Capital gains tax

Under the UK tax regime, capital gains tax is payable on the profit made, less certain sales costs, from the sales of assets. There is an annual allowance of tax-free chargeable gains. Losses can be offset against gains and losses unused in one year can be offset against gains in future years, providing the loss is notified to HMRC within four years of the loss being made. Further information is available from HMRC (www.hmrc.gov.uk).

No capital gains tax is payable on profits made within an ISA or a SIPP.

Cash

Cash is money held on deposit with banks, building societies and other licensed deposit-takers. Interest rates (if any) can be either fixed or variable. Cash held in such institutions is the only asset whose actual value should not fall (except in the very rare instance of negative interest rates). However, the real value can fall and frequently does fall when inflation is higher than the interest rate applying to the account.

Derivatives

Derivatives are tradable securities whose value is dependent, directly or indirectly, on the cash price of an underlying asset such as a share or a bond. Options, futures and covered warrants are examples of derivatives.

Discounted cash flow (DCF)

DCF is used to translate future values into today's values by using, as a discount rate, your specified rate of return. It is the reverse procedure from using a compound growth rate to project a future value from today's value.

For example, if you wanted to project the future value of £100 in two years' time at a compound growth rate of 20% p.a., you would use the following formula: £100 x 1.2 x 1.2 = £144. If you wanted to calculate the net present value of £144 received in two years' time you would reverse the process. If you used the same 20% as a discount rate, the formula would be £144 x (100÷120) x (100÷120) = £100. However, if you applied a lower discount rate, say 10% p.a., the net present value of £144 would be higher: £144 x (100÷110) x (100÷110) = £119 rather than £100.

DCF is widely used in investment appraisals, where it is necessary to calculate the present value of an investment which has costs and revenues spread over several years.

Dividend/dividend yield/dividend cover

A *dividend* is a payment made by a company as a return to its shareholders on their investment in the company. Dividends are normally paid in cash but they can sometimes be paid in the form of additional shares (scrip dividends). Most companies pay an interim dividend, sometime during their financial year, and a final dividend, which is announced at the time of the full year's results. Some large companies pay a quarterly dividend.

The *dividend yield* quoted in most share data services is the dividend paid for the latest financial year expressed as a percentage of the current share price. The dividend used for the calculation is the dividend actually paid by the company, which is currently deemed to be net of basic rate tax (10% for dividends). Normally the dividend used to calculate the dividend yield is the total of dividends for the last financial year, including final dividends which have been declared but not yet paid. However, some yield calculations make adjustments for any changes in interim dividends which have been declared for the current financial year.

When a share price goes *ex-dividend* it means that the buyer of the share is not entitled to receive a dividend which has been declared but not yet paid. The dividend is retained by the seller. The ex-dividend date is important for trading in equity derivatives and spread trades. A *prospective* dividend yield normally refers to the total dividend expected to be paid for the current financial year, expressed as a percentage of the current share price. Hence, the dividend yield percentage goes up when the share price goes down and vice versa.

Dividend cover is the ratio of the company's earnings to its dividend. This cover is commonly used to assess the ability of a company to maintain or increase its dividend in the future. Low dividend covers are therefore normally associated with high dividend yields, and vice-versa.

Earnings/earnings yield

A company's *earnings* are broadly its net profits after tax. Another measure of earnings is EBIT – earnings before interest and tax. Earnings include both cash and non-cash items (e.g. depreciation) and can be massaged to present the company in a favourable light. A study of the company's report and accounts should reveal the extent of the massaging, except when the company's directors have been dishonest, fraudulent or negligent.

The *earnings yield* is the inverse of the price earnings (PE) ratio. It is the earnings per share, i.e. earnings divided by the number of shares (normally for the last financial year), expressed as a percentage of the share price.

Equities

Another name for shares.

Exchange-traded fund (ETF)

ETFs are investment funds which trade on stock exchanges. The funds can hold various assets. The ones relevant to this book are those which hold UK equities. ETFs in the FTSE 100 and FTSE 250 aim to replicate the performance of these indices before charges. They are growing in popularity because:

- They generally have a low cost structure.

- They pay regular dividends.

- Unlike unit trusts and OEICs, you know the price at which you are trading. The spread between the buy and sell price is normally very narrow.

- There is currently no stamp duty payable on ETF investments.

FTSE 100 index

The FTSE 100 index, which commenced in 1984, is the most widely used barometer of the UK stock market. The index includes the top 100 UK shares by market value (price of each share multiplied by the number of shares) and accounts for around 81% of the value of the UK stock market. The index is calculated from the share prices of the top 100 companies, weighted by the total market value of each company.

FTSE 250 index

This is the index of the next top 250 shares, weighted by market value, after the FTSE 100. The index, which commenced in 1986, is calculated in a similar way to the FTSE 100 and accounts for about 15% of the market value of the UK stock market.

FTSE All-Share index

This index comprises companies in the FTSE 100 index, the FTSE 250 index and the FTSE Small Cap index.

Gearing (also known as leverage)

Gearing is normally referred to in the context of derivative contracts. It is a way of increasing exposure to the movement of the contract market price. For example, a gearing of 7 means that the profit (or loss) on a contract will be 7 times as large as the movement of the contract market price. If the contract price increases 1%, your profit will increase 7%. The gearing on spread trades is determined by the number of pounds per point chosen (see Strategy 5).

Gilts

Gilts are bonds issued by the UK government to raise funds. Most have fixed redemption dates, i.e. dates on which the government repays the face value of the gilt. There are two types of gilts:

1. **Index-linked gilts**, where both the interest and the price at which the capital will be redeemed are adjusted to take account of movement in the Retail Prices Index (RPI).

2. **Ordinary gilts**, where the interest rate is fixed in relation to the original face (par) value of the gilt.

148

After their primary issuance, both types of gilts trade on the secondary market. If interest rates have risen above the level pertaining when the gilt was issued (and on which the interest rate is set), the gilt will normally trade below its issue value. There are two types of yield calculation for ordinary gilts:

1. **Current yield**: annual interest payment expressed as a percentage of the current market price.

2. **Gross redemption yield**: includes the annual interest payment but also takes into account the gain or loss to be made on redemption date by comparing the current market price with the redemption value and also taking into account the time to redemption. Adjustments are made to market prices to take into account pending interest payments.

Inflation

Inflation is the annual rate at which prices are increasing. Positive inflation is a measure of the declining purchasing power of money. Very occasionally there is negative inflation, which measures the increasing purchasing power of money when prices are falling.

In the UK, there are various measures of inflation, depending on the selection of goods and services for which the prices are measured. The standard measure of inflation used to be the Retail Prices Index (RPI), but UK governments have increasingly used the Consumer Price Index (CPI) as their preferred measure.

It is no coincidence that the CPI is normally lower than the RPI – as a result, the use of this measure maximises tax revenues and minimises what the government has to pay out in inflation-linked benefits. The CPI excludes major items of expenditure incurred by most households – e.g. mortgage interest.

As I am more concerned with maximising the real market value of your savings than in using inflation measures which have been devised for political purposes, I have used the RPI All Items Index to calculate the real returns of the strategies covered in this book.

Intrinsic value

In the context of this book, intrinsic value is a calculation of the real current investment value of a share or index. Intrinsic value contrasts with the current market price, which is the price at which the share or index is trading at a particular moment in time.

Individual savings account (ISA)

ISAs are UK savings accounts which are free from income tax and capital gains tax. There are two types of ISAs – Cash ISAs and Stocks and Shares ISAs.

Within a Stocks and Shares ISA, dividend income is free from higher rate tax but you cannot reclaim the basic rate tax deducted at source on dividends. Cash interest in a Stocks and Shares ISA is also subject to basic rate tax (but not higher rate tax). Unlike SIPPs, there is no tax relief granted on funds invested in an ISA. However there is no tax deducted on any cash withdrawn from an ISA.

Momentum/relative momentum

In share investing, momentum is the pace at which a share or index price is rising or falling. There are various ways of measuring this momentum, including moving averages (see below). Relative momentum is the pace of movement in a share price compared with, for example, its industry sector or the market as a whole.

Various short-term trading strategies incorporate momentum, as momentum can be a good indicator of future short-term price movement. However, momentum is not normally a good indicator of future long-term price movement.

Moving averages

Moving averages smooth out day-to-day price fluctuations with the aim of showing the price trend. There are different ways to calculate moving averages. We need only concern ourselves with the simple moving average in this book. This is the sum of prices over a specific number of days, divided by that number of days. Moving averages are normally plotted as lines on a graph. Several of the internet sources mentioned in this book will create moving average graphs online from parameters which you set.

Some trading systems use two different moving averages (e.g. 50-day and 90-day) to detect turning points in the market, where the two lines cross.

OEICs (open-ended investment companies)

To an investor, OEICs are very similar to unit trusts. They are collective investments in which you purchase shares rather than units, and the share prices are determined by the net asset values of the companies. The initial charges, management fees and range of funds are very similar to those of unit trusts and you can also only deal on a forward pricing basis. The main difference is that there is only one dealing price for an OEIC and therefore no bid/offer spread.

However, there are sometimes penalties for early redemption of the shares once purchased.

Retail Prices Index (RPI)

See Inflation.

Risk premium

In the context of this book, the risk premium is the extra return demanded by investors for accepting the greater risk of investing in a share as opposed to investing in a gilt, which is virtually risk-free, if you ignore inflation and hold the gilt to redemption. Normally, the risk premium is expressed as an additional percentage return required for each year of investment. My Market Valuation System accounts for the risk premium by dividing the total future projected investment value in five years' time by 1, plus the risk premium divided by 100. On this basis, 10 has been tested to be the appropriate risk premium for a five-year investment in the FTSE 100.

The risk premium required for an individual company investment is much harder to assess. Whilst, barring Armageddon, you will not lose all your investment in a FTSE 100 ETF, your investment in an individual company, even a FTSE 100 company, could become worthless.

Redemption

See Gilts.

Shares

Shares are issued by companies to raise funds as an alternative to borrowing money. A company can issue various types of shares, with different rights and obligations, but the most commonly traded share is the *ordinary share.*

A company may, but is not obliged to, pay regular dividends to ordinary shareholders as a return on their investment. The company's ability to pay dividends is heavily influenced by the earnings which it makes.

If a company is wound up, the shareholders will share the residual value of the company (if any), after all its debts and obligations have been met, in proportion to the number of shares which they hold.

Self-invested personal pension (SIPP)

SIPPs enable individuals to build up personal pension funds with tax-free growth. There are also tax incentives for SIPP investments. Withdrawals from SIPPs cannot be made until a pension is drawn from the SIPP. I discuss SIPPs in more detail in *How to Value Shares and Outperform the Market*. The rules are complicated and so you should consult a professional pensions adviser before investing in a SIPP.

SIPPs could be a very useful vehicle for some of your investments. You can hold a wide range of investments in a SIPP.

Spread

The spread is the difference between the buying and selling price of a trade. It can be expressed in absolute or percentage terms. In spread trading, the spread is expressed in points. So if the buying price of a FTSE 100 contract is 6310 and the selling price is 6306, the spread is 4 points.

Spread trades (also known as spread bets)

Financial spread trades are high-risk investments. As far as UK equities are concerned, you can place a trade on the future price movement of a UK share or of the FTSE 100. At any one time there is a buy price and a sell price, with a spread in between. The spread is the profit of the spread trade provider. This spread is similar to the spread between the buy and sell price provided by a market maker of a share, but it also covers the commission of the spread trading firm. If you buy at the prevailing buy price and subsequently sell at the prevailing sell price, your profit (or loss) is the difference between the two prices multiplied by the amount of stake which you have traded for each point of price movement.

One of the reasons why spread trades are high-risk is that you can use heavy leverage – i.e. get an exposure to the market which is many times greater than the amount of cash which you have to deposit initially. This leverage magnifies profits and losses greatly.

At the time of writing, spread trade profits are not subject to capital gains tax.

Technical analysis

Technical analysis seeks to predict future price movements from past price movements and, in some cases, from trading volumes. See *Value investing* below.

Tracker fund

An equity tracker fund aims to reproduce the performance of an index, such as the FTSE 100, as closely as possible. The fund achieves this tracking by buying the constituent shares of the index in proportion to their weighting within the index. Tracker funds generally have lower costs than actively managed funds because there is no research or decision-making required in the selection of companies within the fund.

Unit trusts

Unit trusts are collective investments in which investors buy units. The price of each unit reflects the number of units in issue and the net asset value of the trust. Unit trusts are established for different markets and products so that investors can gain exposure to the security group of their choice (e.g. UK Smaller Companies).

In addition to buy/sell spreads, unit trusts normally have initial charges of around 5%, although much of this charge can be avoided by buying through a discount broker. The management fees of actively managed funds (as opposed to index-tracking funds) are around 1.5% p.a., with other costs increasing total annual costs to at least 1.8% p.a. In addition to these high charges, what I most dislike about unit trusts is the fact that you can only deal once a day, and then only on a forward basis so that you never know the price at which you are dealing. This is not a recipe for smart investment decisions.

Value investing

Value investing is the polar opposite of investing on the basis of technical analysis. Value investors believe that fundamental financial and other factors determine whether the share price of a company offers good value or poor value and, therefore, whether the share price is likely to increase or decrease. Value investors generally have a medium to long-term investment horizon, since it can sometimes take three or more years for a company's share price to reach fair value.

Volatility

Volatility is a measure of how much a share price moves in relation to the market as a whole. Some share prices are fairly stable and others move all over the place. A share's volatility is normally measured by beta. If a share has a beta of 1.3, it is 30% more volatile than the market. If it has a beta of 0.8, it is 20% less volatile than the market. High volatility is normally associated with high risk, and vice-versa.

Lightning Source UK Ltd.
Milton Keynes UK
UKHW020616140719
346039UK00003B/99/P

9 780857 194626